RAY CHAVARRIA'S
INDIAN FAMILY ROOTS

RAY CHAVARRIA'S INDIAN FAMILY ROOTS

Ray Chavarria

To order additional copies of this book, contact:
Xlibris Corporation
1-888-795-4274
www.Xlibris.com
Orders@Xlibris.com
39825

To my lovely wife,
Margarita Perea Chavarria

Chapter 1

In this chapter, Ramon tells how he started his family history and how he became aware that his parents were of Apache ancestry. Ramon starts his family genealogy from his parents' forefathers, including his father's first family by Dolores Amado.

I, Ramon Chavarria, having been born of good parents, was taught all the learnings of my father, having seen many afflictions in the course of my days. Nevertheless, we have been blessed many times. I write the history of my family, the Chavarrias. This history comes by way of family stories, National Archives records, personal knowledge of family history, and the help of Father John Ancharski, who is a Jesuit priest in Solomon Jesuit priest of Our Lady of Guadalupe Catholic Church in Solomon, Arizona. Father John, as I call him, has provided me with church documents of our family in Solomon. I owe Father John my deepest respect and honor to have known him personally. May Heavenly Father and our Lord Jesus Christ bless him for his kind hand.

My parents were of Indian ancestry (San Carlos Apache of Arizona). My father was born at Solomonville, Arizona, on the 25 January 1882, Graham County. He was baptized on the 28 December 1882 at Our Lady of Guadalupe Catholic Church in Solomonville. He was given the name Pablo Montoya Chavarria. Pablo Chavarria is the son of Francisco Chavarria and Refugia Montoya Chavarria, Mescalero Indian of New Mexico. Francisco is the son of Gregorio Chavarria and Maria Francisca Miera Chavarria, both Mescalero Apache Indians. Francisco was born 26 September 1843. He was baptized as Jose Francisco, the legitimate son of Gregorio and Maria Francisca, at Warm Springs, Ojo Caliente, Taos County. Francisco's paternal grandparents are Eulogio Chavarrilla and Maria Dolores Garcia. His maternal grandparents are listed as Francisco Miera and Maria Dolores Sanchez. Our father, Pablo, married Dolores Conteras Amado on 19 July 1906 at Solomonville, Arizona. Dolores Amado Chavarria was born in 1885 at Altan, Sonora, Mexico. Dolores was Jewish Mexican. She became Catholic when she married our father. This is what my father told me in 1973 before his death. She passed away on 14 December 1920, at Solomonville, Arizona. She gave birth to three girls and five boys in Solomonville, Arizona, namely

Refugia, born on 3 April 1907; Beatriz, born on 6 August 1908; Pablo, born on 25 October 1909; Ernesto, born on 8 February 1911; Rafael, born on 1 April 1914; Antonia Dolores, born on 4 June 1915; Alfredo, born on 28 July 1919; and Manuel, born on 23 November 1920. Dolores Amado Chavarria passed away on December 14, 1920, of breast cancer and her youngest son, Manuel, passed away on June 20, 1921. Little Manuel lived only seven months after his mother's death.

My father, after the death of his wife, Dolores, met my mother and married her nine months after his first wife passed away. My mother, Rita Soto Moreno Chavarria, was born on March 28, 1900, at the San Carlos Apache Indian Reservation called San Pedro at that time. Now it is known as Dudleyville, Arizona. That portion of the reservation was ceded out by the United States federal government in 1902, making my mother, Rita Moreno Chavarria, an Apache woman. My mother was twenty-one years old when she married my father Pablo. As one can see that both parents are from Indian heritage, thus making his first children part Indian and part Jewish. My mother, Rita, became Dolores's children's stepmother. Here she was at age twenty-one when she married our father and inherited seven children to take care of. My mother, Rita, took care of them like they were her own children. My mother was just five years older than Cuca (Refugia). Both used to dress up and go to the town of Solomonville. The men thought that they were sisters. So they tried to date both of them. Cuca told me in Scottsdale, Arizona, before she passed away, that father would get upset with my mother because he would come home and not find her there cooking supper. She called me Monchie (This is my nickname since I was a little boy. My mother gave me that name and it has stayed with me since then), and said, "Rita and I would look at each other and laugh at what we experienced in town, men flirting with us and trying to get a date thinking that we were sisters." Then mother started to have children of her own besides taking care of the children of Dolores and Dad. The first to be born was Roberto Moreno, born on May 19, 1923, in Tempe, Arizona, and was followed by Rudolpho Moreno Chavarria, born on March 12, 1925, Tempe, Arizona; Ramon Moreno Chavarria, born on November 8, 1927, Tempe, Arizona; Jose Josefa Moreno Chavarria, born on March 18, 1930, Tempe, Arizona; and Antonio Moreno Chavarria, born on February 16, 1934, Tempe, Arizona.

Our family history starts in New Mexico, in or about 1720, when California, Utah, Colorado, Nuevo Mexico ("New Spain"), and Texas were under Mexico territories. My great-grandfather on my father side of the family starts with Juan Chavarria, who was a War Chief of the Maricopa Arizona Indians, had a son named Juan Jose Chavarria. Juan Jose became the Pima Indian chief who, with his father Juan Chavarria, defeated the

Chechens of Yuma, Arizona, on the last Indian Wars among the Indians in 1858. He had a son named Gregorio Francisco Chavarria, who was married to Francisca Miera Chavarria. Francisco became known as "White Mountain Apache Coyotero Chief El Fresco," named after the Fresco River in Warm Springs that flows into the Gila River. Francisco also became known by the European as "Francisco the Butcher." Gregorio and Francisca had a son born to them at Ojo Caliente, also known as the Warm Springs Apache Indian Reservation. Francisco was born in the year 1843; rode with Indian chief Cochise, Indian chief of all the Apache tribes of New Mexico and the Arizona territory after the killing of his father at Fort Goodwin in 1865. My great-grandfather Francisco "the Butcher" was a friend to Chief Cochise. They plundered the goods from the Mexicans across the Mexican border and my great-grandfather also came to the aid of Chief Cochise at the cienega in 1864. This made him a war criminal because he fought against the United States Cavalry.

Chapter 2

R amon, great-grandson of Coyotero Chief Francisco "the Butcher," finds out how his great-grandfather was killed by United States Cavalry stockade sentries while he was in prison as a United States war criminal at Fort Goodwin in 1865.

I found out all this information on our family roots search government and state and city records. I found out through the United States Archives in Washington that our great-grandfather was born in Ojo Caliente of the Warm Springs Apache Reservation. The Warm Springs Apaches were at that time under the leadership of Chief Gregorio; after the death of Chief Gregorio, another great chief took over. Nana was a brilliant war chief. He could outsmart the Mexican troops and the United States Cavalry. This is prior to the Treaty of Guadalupe Hidalgo of 1848 and the Gadsden Purchase Treaty of 1853 with Mexico. The United States defeated Mexico and made a land deal to help Mexico get out of debt. The United States bought the land from Mexico that was north above the Gila River in Arizona in 1848, then in 1853 the United States bought the land south from the Gila to the Mexican border as it stands now. The strip of land that was bought is known today as the southern part of Arizona and New Mexico. Indian chief Francisco was given 2,400 acres of agricultural land in the northern and southern portion of the Gila River in Arizona. When great-grandfather was murdered by the white-eye calvary soldiers at Fort Goodwin, his land became an inheritance to his two sons, Francisco and Regino. Francisco was the older of his sons. Regino was the younger. Grandfather Francisco had a daughter named Carmen. Carmen was born at Las Cruces, New Mexico, on 25 October 1868. Then in 1880, Francisco was born at Solomonville, Arizona, on January 25, 1882. Our father, Pablo Montoya Chavarria, was born at Solomonville, Arizona.

Chapter 3

This is the beginning of the Chavarria Indian history, the friendship of Francisco "El Fresco" with Cochise, Indian chief of all Apaches, how Indians received their Spanish names, and how the son of Francisco "El Fresco" happened to become one of the Cochise warriors.

Now that I have given the genealogy of my family roots, I will commence giving our family history with what can be remembered by my older brothers and sisters. Even though I have written the background history of my great-great-grandfather Juan Chavarria down the line to our father Pablo, this was all news to the family. The older members of the family had a very vague recollection that in some way we had Indian blood in us. The older brothers and sisters thought that they had Spanish and Mexican blood, but not Indian. My brothers and sister from father's second marriage to our mother Rita knew that we had Indian blood through her. We used to hear our mother talking the Apache language with one of our neighbors who was also Indian. Her name was Beatrice Estrada; we called her Bee. Later she married and became Mrs. Beatrice Flores. Bee was mother's best friend. They grew up together as children. How they came together to be neighbors as grown-ups, I don't know. My mother told my older brother Roberto that she got her Spanish name when she was baptized in the Catholic church as a little baby. She said to my brother Roberto that our fathers and mothers had no choice but to baptize their children or else they would be taken away someplace where the families couldn't find them. In other words, they were forced into the Catholic religion. After the death of his father, Francisco (our grandfather), became a warrior to Chief Cochise since his father, Francisco "Chief of the White Mountain Coyotero," was a good friend of the chief. Both Indian chiefs went on raids and plunder the Mexicans out of their cattle, household goods, and small children, whom they sold as housekeepers to the Spanish families in New Mexico.

Our great-grandfather broke his friendly relations with Cochise in 1864, because the Coyotero tribe under our great-grandfather Francisco

"El Fresco," or the Butcher, were being blamed for all the killings done to the white settlers on their ranches and stagecoaches; killing all women, children, and men. The Coyoteros were innocent of all this. Francisco had a powwow with Chief Cochise, and they could not come to an agreement and broke relation with each other.

Chapter 4

Geronimo escapes from San Carlos. Francisco, grandfather to Ramon, goes after Geronimo to persuade him to come back to the reservation. Francisco goes all the way to Tempe, Arizona, to find Geronimo. Finding Geronimo had gone from Tempe, Francisco stays with his warriors at the Hayden Casa Viega.

Our older brother Paul told me that our grandmother Refugia talked to him concerning his grandfather Francisco. How he loved to ride his horse and go hunting on the hills after rabbits. She told him, "Your grandfather could ride his horse facing the rear of the horse and shoot his arrows at the rabbits and kill them. He even went after mountain lions that would come at night and kill our cattle and chickens for food. He would track them all night and day until he found that mountain lion and kill him." Grandfather was also good with a rifle and a six-shooter. Paul told me he would have been considered a sharpshooter in these days. I said he must have been real good at what he went after. Paul said to me, "Monchie, our grandfather was a good horseman. That horse he had, Grandma told me that he took him as a little colt and trained him to where that horse could just feel your grandpa's knees and know what Francisco wanted him to do. That horse was like a human being with your grandfather. He would come early in the morning to our bedroom window and wake up Francisco. Francisco loved that horse."

My father told me this story about Geronimo and our grandfather Francisco. "Son," he said, "my father became a warrior to Cochise after the death of my grandfather Francisco at fort Goodwin in 1865. Your great-grandfather was shot like an animal at the hands of those white soldiers. He was put into the fort stockade as a prisoner of war. My grandfather went to the rescue of Chief Cochise when they had him trapped in the cienega plateau running out of ammunition. He went in and saved Cochise and his warriors, thus making him a war criminal. This is why they put him in the stockade." I will find out later how all this came to be. My father did not know by what Indian name his grandfather was known. Then he said to me, "Son, my father rode with a band of Cochise warriors after the renegade Geronimo, who broke away from the San Carlos Indian

Reservation and took to the warpath again killing any white gentile that they would find." Geronimo had a very deep hate for the Mexicans, since they slaughtered his wife, his children, and his mother-in-law. That day of the slaughter, Geronimo was on his way to have a powwow with the United States Cavalry concerning making peace. When he came back, he found his family murdered. After that, Geronimo didn't care how many Mexicans or whites they would kill. He was out to avenge their death one way or the other. Geronimo kept his word until he surrendered to the U.S. Cavalry. Our grandfather went after Geronimo and his group under the orders of Cochise. Cochise wanted Francisco to go after Geronimo to persuade him and his warriors to come back to the San Carlos Reservation. This search brought our grandfather all the way to Hayden's crossing, what is known as Tempe, Arizona. According to my father, when my grandfather arrived at the Hayden crossing, they found out that Geronimo's warriors had already left the area. Our grandfather went up the butte (Tempe Butte) and saw the renegade Indians on their way south heading to Mexico. Francisco and his warriors decided to rest overnight because they found it impossible to catch up with them. My father looked at me and said, "Son, they stayed at the Casa Viega." The Casa Viega is on the west corner of First and Mill avenues. It is still standing and has been remodeled to a restaurant known today as Monty Steak House. Father then tells me, "My father left his name on one of the walls inside the old Hayden building, the Casa Viega." I found out that what he said was true because I saw the name "FRANCISCO" carved on one of the walls inside. Some of my friends and I went swimming at the Tempe swimming pool at night; afterward, we went inside this old structure to play. We lit some old papers to make a fire, and we saw that name on the wall. I told my father about that, and he said that his father was taught by a Mormon rancher how to write his name. That's all he knew how to write. I do remember that I was about twelve years old and at that time, I did not know that Francisco was my father's father. We, the younger Chavarrias, thought all the time that Blas Ortiz was our grandfather because our father, Pablo, always mentioned his name as his father. So we called him grandfather too. We didn't know that "Blas" was our grandmother's second husband after the death of our real grandfather, Francisco.

Chapter 5

Ramon takes his wife, Margarita Perea Chavarria, to Tempe's Monty Steak House. Ramon talks to the Casa Viega manager about the name Francisco carved on one of the walls. The manager tells Ramon that the name is still there, but the walls have been plastered.

In 1995, I took my wife to visit her sister Maria Perea Barriga who lives in Tempe, Arizona. After we had been there for a week, I took my wife, Margarita, to eat steak at Monty's Steak House, better known to all the Tempe senior citizens as the old Casa Viega. I met the manager of Monty's and we started a conversation concerning Tempe's history. I introduced myself and he asked me if I had resided in Tempe before moving to San Diego, California. I related some of my youth background concerning my swimming at the Tempe swimming pool. How we used to sneak at night after the pool was clean for the next day. He then asked me, "Why did you kids have to sneak in at night to swim?" This is when I told him how Mexicans or anyone that was not white was prohibited from swimming with the white. I said we were plainly discriminated by the white people of Tempe. He could not believe that something like this could have happened in Tempe. Then he told me, "Ray, in this restaurant, we do not discriminate, especially minorities. They are U.S. citizens like me and are entitled to the protection of our Constitution." I thanked him for his kind remarks. Then I mentioned to him about my grandfather's name on one of these walls. He told me that before they plastered the adobe walls, the workers saw the name "Francisco" carved on the wall. One of the cement plasters brought it to his attention. He then said to me, "Ray, if I would have known the history of that name, I would have put a glass cage to protect the name. This is Arizona history. Would it be all right if we find the name of your grandfather Francisco on the wall, if we put a glass cage to protect the name and a little write-up how the name came to be written on the wall?" I gave him permission to do so. I don't know if he did what he told me he was going to do. I haven't been to Tempe since then. I really don't know if he did removed the plaster and made that glass cage he told me he was going to do. I want the family to know at this time our father had not mentioned anything concerning his Indian heritage. My father told me about being an

Indian in 1973. He was recuperating from surgery in the city of Tempe. The genealogy in chapter 1 was compiled by me, Ramon, by searching federal, state, archives record, including Arizona towns like Solomon and Safford, Tempe, Phoenix, the Indian reservations of San Carlos, White Mountain, Maricopa, and the New Mexico Indian pueblos.

Chapter 6

Ramon's father tells him about his father, Francisco, how he became domesticated, the white man's ways. Pablo tells his son Ramon about his father's land inheritance, tells how he and his first family came to Tempe and lived in the Hayden apartments.

Our father never told any of his children that we were Indians of Apache ancestry. That part of our history is revealed to Ramon when I told my father that I was writing the family history. The family has to remember that my father, Pablo Sr., had to go and have surgery done on his right hip because he fell in his trailer home. After having hip surgery, he came down with an infection on his bladder and was operated a week after his hip surgery. I took off from work for two weeks in order that I might go visit our father at the Tempe St. Luke's Hospital. When I told him that I was writing the history of our family, his eyes brighten up and he said to me, "Mijo (meaning son), I am glad that somebody in the family is interested in the history of our family." I said to my father, "We have been instructed in the Church of Jesus Christ of Latter-day Saints that we, as members, must trace our lineage and write a history of our families to leave to our future posterity and to do Temple Ordinance in our behalf for those that have passed to the spirit world." Our father knew what I was talking about. He had studied the Gospel with the Mormon missionaries.

The day that he was to be baptized, Beatrice and a friend from Scottsdale went to our father's house, and Beatrice talked to our father not to get baptize in the Mormon Church. Father told me that Beatrice told him, "Father, we are all Catholics in the family. You will disgrace all of your children if you join the Mormons. Monchie has already disgraced us by joining them." Then he said to me, "Son, I didn't want to create any animosity amongst my children. So I went with them to Scottsdale for the day. That way, the missionaries won't find me at home. When they came at night to find out what had happen to me, I told them the truth, that my daughter was upset with me and that is why I had decided not to be baptized at this time." The missionaries understood, and so did I after he explained things to me. Let me get back to our grandfather Francisco. Our father told me at the hospital this story about his father. "Never in my life did I ever dream that someday I would sleep at the same place my father slept after he was chasing Geronimo to Tempe and stayed at the old Casa Viega here in Tempe."

The Haydens remodeled the whole Casa Viega into family apartments. It had floor rooms and upstairs rooms for rent and they also had a restaurant to feed those that could afford to eat out. Let me tell you how my grandfather finally settled down as the white man wanted the Indians to settle down and become domesticated in their ways. Grandfather became an Indian cultivator farmer and a good one, according to my mother's stories about him. The way I understood my father was that grandfather became a farmer. He planted corn, squash, pinto beans, sugar cane, watermelons, cantaloupes cotton, and hay. He had ranch hands that worked for him at the ranch. People named his ranch El Rancho Grande, "the big ranch." This land that great-grandfather left to his sons was in Safford and Solomon, Arizona. I will return to this land inheritance later. Great-grandfather left three sons instead of two, like the family believed. First, it was Francisco, Trinidad, and Regino. I discovered this in my research into the Chavarria history, plus a killing of one of our family members. This I will write about as I go along in our history.

Chapter 7

Ramon's father discovers how his grandfather was shot by U.S. Cavalry guard sentries at Fort Goodwin. His sons become heirs to his land. Later, this land is taken by the United States government under the Treaty of Guadalupe Hidalgo and the Gadsden Treaty Purchase. Brother Paul tells him about their grandfather knowing the Earp brothers and Doc Holliday. Ramon learns about his great-grandfather being shot, what was written about his death, and how his grandfather met his wife Refugia.

Father told me that his father like the wild ways of the Indians. That is to go hunting on horseback and shoot your game from the horse saddle after your game. "Your grandfather really loved to go hunting for wild game. My mother said to me, 'Pablito, your father was a very smart man. He could track an animal for days and catch up with that animal and kill it for food. That horse of his was so dedicated to him that the horse would have given his life for him.'" After, our grandfather settled down as a domesticated Indian. He started to round up wild horses and break them down from their wild ways. He would sell those horses for a living. Later on, he, grandfather, started a freight hauling business. He had forty oxen and twenty freight wagons. His freight hauling business would take him away from his ranch for months at a time. He had farmworkers taking care of his crops while he was on his business trips. These trips let him go into towns like Bisbee, Arizona, to pick up some ore and haul it to Morenci or to Miami. These mining companies had the ore smelters. The two mining companies were the only ones in Arizona at that time that had the facilities to remove the gold or ore minerals from the dirt. Later on, he started taking other goods to Las Cruces, New Mexico. It was in Las Cruces that he met our future grandmother—Refugia Conteras Montoya, a Mescalero Indian woman. Grandmother was from the Mescalero Apache Indian Reservation.

They married in Las Cruces about 1867 because his first child was born in Las Cruces, New Mexico, in 1868. This happens to be our Tia Carmen. Then he brought our grandmother and his daughter, Carmen, to live in Solomonville, Arizona, where he had his ranch of 2,400 acres that his father left him and his brothers, Trinidad and Regino. When his father was shot to death at Fort Goodwin, Arizona, in 1865 by the United States Cavalry, the *Tucson Sentential Newspaper* had this to say about his shooting.

Death of an Apache chief. Col. Robert Pollock, Commanding at Fort Goodwin, informs General Mason, under date of November 11th of the killing of an Apache Chief of white Mountain Tribe known as "Francisco the Butcher" and who has been notorious for many years in the robberies and murders committed by his Tribe. Francisco was arrested by Captain Kennedy for complicity in the massacre of a German family and others from Texas, on the Cienega, twenty-eight miles from Tucson, on the Apache pass road, a short time since as well as to induce the Tribe to give up three children captured at the time same time massacre who are yet in the Indian's hands, Col. Pollock says, "On the night of the 10th inst, about 10 o'clock, the prisoner applied to the acting Sergeant of the guard, Wm. O Pascoe Corporal of the UE, 1, 1st Cav, for permission to go to the rear, which was granted, and he was accompanied by a Corporal of UE, 1, 1st Cav. C.V., and two men, on arriving at a point, about ninety yards from the guard house, the prisoner, who was a large and splendidly proportioned man, started and sprang off, when the guard fired several shots at him, nearly all of which took effect and he fell dying instantly, shot through the brain and heart and abdomen. I found that the rivets of the shackles on the left leg and hand had been filed off and taken out, completely liberating the prisoner." Francisco's death has made little or no impression on the Indians to the vicinity, they visit the Post daily, and appear to be satisfied that death is the inevitable results of attempts to escape from the guard house, besides the deceased was much feared among them, and it seems that many breath easier now that they have no more to fear him.

My father gave me a different version of his grandfather's killing. This is his side of that story. As told to my father Pablo by his mother, Refugia, "Your grandfather wasn't like the white man wrote about him. He was a very good man with children; he took a concern about them." If he saw a member of the tribe abuse a child in his presence, he would hit that person with his hands and warn him that if he do it again, he would do the same to him but worse. Grandfather had the respect of his tribe members. Yes, they feared him. He was as well built and tall like Chief Cochise. His height was about 6 feet 2 inches and his weight 190 pounds, and he was a very handsome man. He was the only Indian that was equal to Cochise in battle. He was very disciplined in his ways of life. The real reason the white men caught up with him and made him a prisoner of war was not as the white men wrote about him.

Father looked at me with tears in his eyes and said to me, "Son, this is the way your grandfather was caught before going to the rescue of Cochise at the Cienega." My grandfather received notice from one of his scouts that they had Cochise trapped at the Cienega and that his warriors were running out of ammunition. Grandfather called for some warriors to join him in rescuing Cochise. When the U.S. Cavalry saw the warriors of Francisco coming to help Cochise, they took off, and that is how he saved Cochise and his small band of Indians. Because my great-grandfather helped the chief, he became an enemy of the United States of America. After that, the U.S. Cavalry went looking for "Francisco the Butcher," as he was known among the white men. He went into hiding. Sometimes he would hide on the sacred mountain called Graham Mountain today. He would climb all the way to the top of the mountain and could see for miles around. He could tell when the troops would leave his land. There was plenty to eat on that mountain. Bear, wild goats, rabbit, quail, pine nuts, acorn nuts, and plenty of water to drink. Then my father said to me, "Ramon, my father got tired of running and hiding until one day, he called his tribe and told them what he felt would be to the best interest of the family cluster. This was his decision to make in order to save the members of his tribe. They would march to Fort Goodwin together and he would turn himself in to the cavalry soldiers and see what they would do to him. My father was at this time about twenty or twenty-one years old and grandfather Francisco was about forty-seven. After he turned himself in to the cavalry, they stuck him in the guardhouse with iron shackles in both feet and hands. According to my mother telling me this story, the guards would go into the guardhouse and hit him with the butt of their rifles to amuse themselves by beating Francisco and making him moan in pain. She said to me, 'Pablo my son, I went to see him at the Fort and I was frightened by the way he looked. He was so beaten up that he said to me, "I don't think that I'm going to live very long here."

"My mother, Refugia, heard the story of our great-grandfather from her husband, who happened to be the son of Francisco 'the Butcher.'" After the death of his father, Francisco joined Cochise and his tribe until the death of Cochise. After the death of Cochise, he rode with the sons of Cochise, Taza, and Naiche. After the death of Taza, Francisco quit his raiding activities and became domesticated by farming his land. My father said to me, "Son, this is how your great-grandfather was captured. He turned himself in, not captured by the white men." Then my father said to me, "Son, my father had 2,400 acres of land around Safford and

Solomonville in 1868." After the death of his father, my grandfather left all that land to him and his brother Regino. (Please note that at this time my own father did not know that his grandfather had three sons instead of two.) This land was left to our grandfather and his brother Regino by their father, our great-grandfather. We haven't found out how he became owner of all this land. We believe that at that time, Indians could claim as much land as they wanted to.

Grandfather, on his ore hauling trips from Bisbee, Arizona, on occasions, would go through Tombstone, Arizona, the town too tough to die. Grandfather would stay for a few days to give his crew and the oxen a time to rest before they continued on their journey to deliver the minerals they were hauling to Morenci, Arizona, to be sweltered into ore bars. Our grandfather knew Wyatt Earp and his brothers, Virgil and Morgan. This back history is told to Tony and me by our older brother Paul (Pablo Jr.) before his death. Paul said to us, "Let me tell you two a true story that happened in our family. Our grandfather was much liked in Tomestone by the Earp brothers. The Earp brothers took care of grandfather while he and his crew were camping outside of town of Tombstone. On one occasion, some drunk cowboy wanted to gunfight grandfather. Grandfather never carried a gun or rifle into town. When the Earp brothers heard what was happening to Francisco, they went to his rescue and that Doc Holliday was with them also.

Grandmother told Paul that grandfather was very well-liked by the people in Tombstone who knew him, simply because he minded his own business and kept his thoughts to himself of anything that was not right in town.

Chapter 8

Ramon learns from his father, Pablo, the business that his father was involved with and his farmland, how he happened to get the land, and how the family lost it. The government creates the White Mountain Apache Reservation and later the San Carlos Apache Reservation. The federal government leaves him and his family inside the San Carlos Indian Reservation.

On one of his trips from Bisbee to Morenci to take his freight wagons load to the smelter, his oxen came down sick with cholera. One by one, they started to die on the trail. Grandfather, instead of waiting and watching his animals die, gave instructions to his crew to wait for his return. He got on his horse, took off to Morenci, and bought mules to finish his hauling the ore he had contracted to do—deliver that ore to the Morenci smelter. Grandfather never again did use oxen to haul any loads. He stayed with mules from that day on. The wagon master of his mule train was his son-in-law Jesus Sainz, who was married to his daughter Carmen. Carmen Chavarria was twenty-one years old and Jesus was forty-eight. Jesus at times served as the constable of Solomonville. He was six feet tall and weighed about two hundred pounds. My father told me that Jesus was a very mean man. He was a good rifleman and could also shoot a revolver pretty good. The cowboys were afraid of him. So they didn't cause any problem in town.

Jesus was previously married and had a son named Gabriel. His wife passed away two years before he came to work for grandfather as his wagon master. Grandfather took a liking to Jesus, and Jesus married our aunt Carmen around 1887. Our aunt Carmen was twenty-one years old and Jesus's son, Gabriel, was almost eighteen years old. I will continue their history later on because I feel that I need to continue my father's history before I continue on anybody else's history.

When, Pablo moved from Solomonville to Tempe with the family in 1921, he rented an apartment at the old Casa Viega. Mr. Carl Hayden had two daughters named Sally and Betty, and they remodeled the place as apartments and a restaurant. Paul, our brother, explains this better in his own words later on his own personal history of Tempe at the Tempe

Historical Museum in Tempe, Arizona. Paul gave me a copy of his story to keep. I will turn into his history later on to bring what he remembers of the past. Pablo, our father, told me this family history. When they moved to Tempe from Solomon, he was working as a railroad hand for the Southern Pacific Railroad Company. He played on Saturdays and Sundays at the Casa Viega restaurant for the Hayden sisters. Later on, Paul and Ralph played at the restaurant for a dollar a night. My sisters Cuca and Beatrice waited on tables for a dollar also, plus the tips they would be given by the patrons of the restaurant.

My father never thought that someday he would be living on the place in Tempe that his own father stayed overnight at the Casa Viega when his father made the trip to see if he could persuade Geronimo to go back to the San Carlos Reservation.

My father moved from the Hayden apartments (La Casa Viega) to the railroad section that was on the corner of Eighth Street and Farmers, near the railroad tracks. My father used to play with his band on the weekends. He played the violin like nobody did that I have ever known. He played that instrument so good that he almost made the violin talk. He was that good. He taught others concerning music. My father was a man that loved music and the way he taught it was by teaching the person to be able to read the music scale or music notes. He taught his boys music including me, but I didn't feel anything by playing the saxophone. I would rather dance to the music than play it. My father noticed one day that I was paying more attention to the kids outside playing games, and he said, "Son, you go outside and play with your friends." I got up from my chair and went outside to play and that was the end of my music lessons. I'll say this though. I always went to the dances where my father and my brothers played. I could see my father's face with a smile as I danced on the dance floor. On their intermissions, he would come and sit with me on the table and just visit me. Yes, he would ask if the music sounded all right. I was very honest with him and I would answer yes or no. If I answered no, he would ask me why. Then I would tell him that one of the musicians sometimes would miss his note. Then he would say to me, "You're right because I've been hearing him make those mistakes tonight. I'm going to have a talk with him later on if he continues to make those mistakes again."

Father was very considerate with his musician. He would give them a chance to correct themselves on learning the proper way of playing instead of playing by ear. If they didn't improve, then he would get rid of him and get another in his place. I'll say this about father, I can remember that I saw him just get rid of two persons in his entire musical career. His group lasted about fifty-two years together professionally in Arizona. My father's band was known throughout Arizona as "Los Chavarrias." They played in the mining towns such as Morenci, Globe, Bisbee, Solomon, Safford, Superior, Casas Grandes, Scottsdale, Phoenix, and many more towns in Arizona. As long as I can remember, my father's band played at every "Fiestas Patrias" in Tempe. This is the day that Mexicans celebrate their independence from Spain, on the 15-16 of September every year. This Mexican tradition is still celebrated every year. On the fiestas, they have food stands where they sell Mexican foods like chili con carne, beef/pork/corn tamales, cheese/beef enchiladas, bean tacos, plus other Mexican goodies. They have dances of old kinds throughout the fiesta activities for that day. Then at night, a big dance is held for those who want to enjoy the night, dancing to various type of music. My father's band was one of the main band at this function every year. Until he retire from playing music at the age of eighty-seven.

It was during his hospital stay that he told me about his father's land taken away by the United States government. I ask, "What land, father?" Then he said to me, "Listen carefully, my son, in what I am about to tell you. Your great grandfather left my father and Uncle Regino, 'twenty-four hundred acres' of land that his tribe donated to him. This land was on both sides of the Gila River starting from Safford, Arizona, all the way to San Jose, Arizona. The land left to my father, he tells me, was also left to his brother Regino. In 1871, the United States government took the upper portion of his land, from the Gila River, heading north. They made an Indian reservation called the White Mountain Apache Reservation. Then again in 1872, they took the bottom of his land to add to the White Mountain Apache Reservation. They called it the San Carlos Apache Reservation Addition. This was my father's south portion of his land, leaving him with nothing. They took a survey from the center of the Gila River down fifteen miles. This left the family inside of the San Carlos Apache Reservation. Francisco, your grandfather, Grandmother Refugia, and your Tia Carmen were living inside of the San Carlos Addition. They left them alone because they were Indians. Then six months after, the government decided to cede part of the north and south part of the reservation starting from Fort Thomas to San Jose, then up to Morenci out of the reservation. This left your grandfather with no land whatsoever. This was 1872 when they ceded this piece of land out of the reservation and started to sell it as preemption land after the land was ceded out. Your grandfather and his family continued to live in his ranch. This we don't understand, son. How did the government get the right to take my father and his brother Regino's land away from them?" At this time, father started to tell me about his Tio Regino.

"My Tio Regino believed that the land belong to them again after it was ceded out. During this time, Tio Regino had become an alcoholic and my father had become a cultivator of the soil. 'Farmer and rancher.' That's when he started his freight hauling business. While your grandfather was working the farm, he had to leave on his freight wagons to pick up some ore or something else. He would be gone for weeks at a time. My Tio would sell some of this land to the Mormons who had come to settle in Safford and the surrounding areas. A Mormon farmer told him to go and do something to save his land because his brother was selling all of his land. Grandfather Francisco loved his brother very much and didn't want to hurt him by telling him to quit his drinking and settle down. Everyone in the family knew that the brothers were the owners of that land. Even after the government took it out or ceded out of the reservation. Since the government did not remove them out of the land, they believed that the land was theirs again, that the government had changed their mind in taking the land from them and now they were returning it back to them.

Chapter 9

Ramon's father, Pablo, tells him about his uncle Regino's drinking habit, how land was obtained in the West from the government, and the conspiracy to get the land from Grandfather Francisco where the government swindled the land out from the Chavarria family.

I mentioned before how our grandfather and Regino had gotten the land of their father, Francisco. The family did not know that our great-grandfather had had three sons. Francisco (our grandfather) first, followed by Tio Trinidad, then Tio Regino. I discovered this later on my investigation of the Chavarria homestead. This is what is known by the Chavarria's concerning Tio Regino: that grandfather loved his little brother Regino very much. But that Regino started to drink hard liquor at an early age and became an alcoholic, womanizer, a liar, and a cheat. Regino spent more time getting drunk than helping grandfather at the ranch with the business at hand. Grandfather at this time had his freight wagon business and his farming. Even though he had some of his tribe working in the ranch, planting and harvesting, Regino didn't care. When he would run out of money, he would go to the Mormons and see who wanted to buy some of his land. This is how he was able to maintain his drinking habit, by selling the family land. Let me mention here that the family still believes that the land was theirs. But it wasn't theirs at all. The government was giving the land away for settlements to those that were coming in to settle as farmers in the West. These pioneers were getting 160 acres of homestead land free. This came under the Homestead Act of 1862, passed by the Congress of the United States of America. Yes, Grandfather Francisco did do something concerning the land to prevent Regino in selling any more land that they own. Our grandfather and grandmother never said anything to the family of what steps they had taken to keep Regino from selling more of the land. As a matter of fact, nobody in the family knew what grandfather did to prevent his brother from selling some more land.

Records in Safford Courthouse, in Safford, Arizona, show that Francisco and Regino had over two thousand acres of land at one time. This area is called Safford Valley today. It runs from Safford to San Jose, Arizona. This happened in the early 1890s. Tio Regino eventually became the owner of all this land. Let me tell my father's side of how Regino came to swindle the land from the Chavarria's, that is, his brother's family—Francisco's wife Refugia, and his children, Blas Ortiz, Carmen, Francisco Jr., and Pablo. "It was a hot summer day in 1891," he began his account of his father's death. "Father was coming to Morenci with a freight wagonload; he had ten wagons being pulled by mules. His son-in-law Jesus Sainz was his wagon master. They left Bisbee with their loads and came on the trail pass they always took, close to the mountains. On the first day, they noticed three Indians following them on the top of the mountains."

"They didn't do anything to show any suspicious mischief. On the third day, the wagons were traveling close to the mountain and they saw the Indians coming down to meet the freight train. My father, Francisco, called Jesus and told him to stay with the wagons. My father headed his horse toward the Indians who were about a mile from the wagons. My father might have thought that they need water or food. When Jesus and the rest of the wagons drivers noticed that my father did not return soon, Jesus and four drivers took off on the mules. As they approached the scene of the meeting of the Indians and my father, they saw his horse standing close to a body on the ground. One of the drivers hollered, 'It's Francisco, he's hurt!' When they got down from their mules, Jesus went over to see what was wrong with his father-in-law. He discovered that Francisco's head had been crutched like his horse had stopped all of a sudden and Francisco went over his horse's head and hit the big boulder with his head and got killed. They put him on one of the wagons and they delivered the body to my mother." But then my father said to me, "Son, I believe that those Indians were not Indians at all. Because one of the drivers said that farther down the trail, they found three pairs of pants and shirts with brown paint powder on them and they had fresh blood on them. It must have been whites dressed as Indians who killed my father." My father looked at me and said to me, "I don't believe that the horse threw him and he hit the rock." This is my father's own version of what he believed his father died of. "I believe that as my father approached them after catching up to them, he got down from his horse to talk to them or he might have been on his saddle. While he was conversing with one of them, he probably noticed that they were not Indians, but one must have gotten behind his back, hit him with the rifle butt, and knocked him down. Then they must have picked him up and hit him against the boulder to make it look like an accident in order to blame the horse throwing him off his saddle." Because this is what happened after the death of grandfather. "Regino came over to the house of my mother, Refugia, and told her that now that Francisco was dead, the property now belongs to him alone. This is what my father related to me concerning this property. "My father had so much land that it took a man half a day to go through the entire land that both he and Regino own. People in that area called it El Rancho Grande, "the big ranch." Don't forget that this is being told to me by my father when he was at the hospital at age ninety-two. My father told me, "Son, pay attention of what I'm going to tell you concerning my father before his death." Then I asked him, "Is it all right with you if I can write all this you're telling me concerning our history?" He said, "Of course you can, son." Then I said to him, "Father, I have to go to my car and bring my notebook so that I may take some of what you're telling about our back history." He then said to me, "Migito (son), here, use this." And he handed me a shopping grocery bag with the name Bashas on it. He had this paper bag on it. He had this paper bag on the side of his wheelchair.

I didn't want to hurt his feelings, so I took the grocery bag and started taking notes. This is what he said to me, "Your grandfather was a friend of Geronimo and Naiche. That at one time in 1873, Geronimo and Naiche were in the reservation at San Carlos, so was his family, Grandmother Refugia and their daughter Carmen and himself. The United States had taken all of his land away and created two Indian reservations, the White Mountain Apache Reservation and the San Carlos Apache Reservation. Father told me, 'the government has ways or laws that if they want your land, they can take it away from you any time they need land for their own purposes.' My father's land was taken at first by some presidential papers under what they call president's executive orders. I don't know what the president has to do with my father's land, but he lost it to them and they let him live on afterward inside the San Carlos Reservation. He told me that Geronimo was a medicine man with very strong spiritual powers. That he could go into battle and the bullets would miss him completely. Geronimo was never wounded in battle against the white man. He was not a chief, the chief of the Chiricahaus was Naiche, son of the late Cochise. He said, after the death of Chief Cochise, his first son became the chief and that was Taza, but he died, and Naiche took his place until him and Geronimo were captured in 1887 in Mexico. Your Tata, (grandfather) he was well acquainted with both Geronimo and Naiche." We must remember that Francisco, our grandfather, rode with Chief Cochise after his father was killed at Fort Goodwin. Then after the death of Cochise, he rode as a warrior with Taza, until his death; then he rode with Naiche until he quit being a warrior and went to his land to farm it.

Chapter 10

Geronimo and Naiche camped at Francisco's land along the Gila River in Solomonville. Francisco used to provide steers for their meat for their raiding journeys. Ramon learns from his father how they dried the meat so it would not spoil on the road to Mexico.

As you can see, grandfather knew Geronimo and Naiche very well and their warriors. I asked my father, "Papa, what do they do with the meat that was left from the steers?"

"They cut it into long strips and hung it on top of the mesquite trees to dry. The meat would be dried by morning, then they would cut it into small pieces and put them into the leather pouches and be on their way. If every thing went fine, they would give my father some of their booties."

I asked what booties are. "The goods that they stole from the Mexican towns across the border."

"Son," he said to me with tears in his eyes, "Geronimo and Naiche like to camp at your grandfather's land because the grass was very good for the horses and the water from the Gila River was clean and fresh to drink. They never threw anything into that water, they buried whatever mess they made and cover it well, so that if the U.S. Cavalry came to your grandfather's land, they could not accuse him of harboring renegade Indians. Our people took good care of my father."

"Did grandfather ever felt like joining them for one more raid?" I asked further.

He said to me, "Your grandfather was a man of his word. When he quit riding with Naiche, he told your grandmother that he would never again go on raids, and he kept his word until they killed him."

My own father hasn't believed the story of how his father, Francisco, was killed. He believed until he died in 1973 that his father was murdered by whites in order to get his land.

Chapter 11

Ramon's father, Pablo, tells Ramon how they lost their ranch land to Tio Regino. Regino promised money to Refugia, his sister-in-law. Regino kept all the money on the sale of the ranch where the Chavarrias and Ortizes lived.

Father and his first family did not know to this day until I showed them the homestead certificate. I'll correct myself here. Our father never knew that his father's land they were living at was really theirs, not Tio Regino's. The family accepts Blas Ortiz as our grandfather. Tio Pancho was ten years old and our father, Pablo, was eight when our real grandfather, Francisco, met that accident on the road to deliver his ore he had contracted to do. Regino played a dirty trick on the family. He told our grandmother that he was going to give her some land to keep as her own, which he did. Our grandmother really thought that Regino was the owner of all this land. She was glad to get the land from Regino. Nobody in the family knew that Regino was caught stealing a steer and was going to go to prison for a few years. He came over to grandmother and told her that he wanted the land back that he had given her. According to my father, Pablo, Tio Regino told our grandmother that he could not sell his portion of the land because the papers included all the land he had given her. That in order to be able to sell he had to include that portion of the land too. This history, my older sister Refugia (Cuca) told me, and this is my father's version.

My father said to me, "Son, my Tio Regino was a liar. He promised my mother that he was going to give her some money out of the sale of the land. He never did. On day in February 1904, a very cold morning, my Tio Regino came over to the ranch. He was accompanied by three lawmen wearing marshal badges. They had in their possession side guns and their rifles in their right hand when they got off their horses. One of them came with Tio Regino walking to the front door of the house and he knocked on the door, and my mother went to the door and opened it and Tio Regino told her that the marshal had some papers for her to vacate the ranch property. They told her that the family had twenty-four hours to leave or else they would go to jail." This happened on February 8, 1904. I will be revealing more on Tio Regino on the land as I go on the family history.

Now I give an account of Blas Ortiz. All of this information really surprised me; to find out that Blas was not our grandfather. The reason for this is that the smaller children didn't know what was going on in the family. The family had a dark secret within the Chavarria and Sainz families.

Chapter 12

Ramon's father, Pablo, tells him how Blas Ortiz came into the family and why Pablo learned to love Blas as his father. Blas received the homestead certificate and kept it hidden all these years for some reason. Ramon finds out who was the one that could have saved the ranch from Regino.

They did not want the rest of the family to know. Our older brothers and sisters never said anything concerning their family history. This is the reason we never knew what happened in the family in the eighteen hundreds. As I started to ask our father questions concerning the history of the Chavarria's, my father smiled at me and said to me, "Mijo [son], sit down close to me and I will tell you all that I can remember about our family. I am very proud of you and happy that at least someone in the family is trying to find our ancestors." He said to me, "I am very glad that you are trying to find your ancestors. Nobody in the family ever tried to find out concerning our family roots. None of my children ever tried to find out where our fathers and mothers came from. That is why I will tell you some dark secrets that have been in the family for years. This I remember very well that after the death of my father, Uncle Regino started to sell part of the land that we were living in. It was a very big ranch, acres and acres as far as the eye could see."

"Since the land was left to both brothers, (please note that at this stage our father only knew that there were only two brothers, not three) Francisco and Regino, my mother married Blas Ortiz who was a ranch hand at our ranch. Blas married my mother Refugia two years after my father's accident. He was a good father and husband to our mother. Blas took the responsibility of managing the ranch. He worked from early morning to late in the evening. Some days, your Tio Pancho and I, we would go to the fields and bring his lunch. He would wash our hands using water from his water canteen. Then he would open his lunch basket and give us a burrito to eat with him under a big cottonwood tree or some other tree. It depended where they were working that day. After lunch, he would play with us for a little while and then he would say, 'Time to go and help your mother at the house.' It wasn't until we grew up that we found out that mother would put those burritos in Blas's lunch basket so we could keep him company while he ate his lunch. My mother at that time believed that she had inherited some of the land being the widow of my father, Francisco. Until one day, Tio Regino came over to the house and told our mother that he was planning to sell the ranch, the part that was his. He had already given to my mother so many acres to keep as hers. A week later, Tio Regino came back to the house and told my mother that he had to take the land back that he had given her. He had some papers with him." Father got a bit upset at this time and said to me, "Son, Tio Regino was nothing but a liar. He promised mother that he had to have her land because the sale of the land had to be all the acres both he and his brother owned. That once he sold it, he would give her part of the money he would receive." Yes, Regino sold the ranch land, but he never gave our grandmother a penny. That is why he, Regino, came to the ranch that cold February morning with three vaqueros wearing law badges. They were given twenty-four hours to clear the ranch. This is why we don't have anything to do with Regino's family. My father then said to me that after they left the ranch, they went to the town of Solomonville to find a place to stay. They found a friend of the family and related to them what had happened to their ranch. This family, by the name of Garcia, had a house on back of theirs; they were welcome to stay there and they didn't have to pay rent because the house needed fixing and they could use that money for repairs. Remember that this was during the winter months in Solomonville and it snows there. The family took great pains in repairing the house against the rains and snow. Grandfather Blas worked on the fields around during the day. After he got home from work, he would eat supper with the family. He would start in fixing the roof, windows, doors, and the roof. Father told me, "Son, father would stay fixing whatever he was doing until he finished. He would work with a lantern to give him light. Sometimes he would work until midnight, get up at five in the morning, and go to work that day. Son, he was a hardworking man and he taught all of us to work hard at whatever we do for someone who was paying us for our labor."

"After the house was repaired because your uncle Pancho and I, we, also helped our father Blas in fixing the house during the day. He would tell my mother what had to be done and how. So we also learned from him how to build a house. After the house was done, your Tio Pancho and myself, we, also went to work around some of the ranches in Solomonville and Safford, as farm labors. During our youth, Tio Pancho and I, we learned to play music. He played the guitar and I the violin. At night, we would take our music instruments and play for Mother and Blas. They would dance to our music and sometimes they would sit with us and sing. My mother was a very good singer. She had a very strong voice. Mother would see that we didn't stay up too long. She would say to us, 'It's time for bed, don't forget you're working tomorrow, and don't forget to say your prayers.'" Then my father said to me, "I married Dolores, my first wife, in 1906. I met Dolores in Tucson, Arizona. I met her at a dance that your uncle Pancho, myself, and other musicians from Solomon went to play at this dance."

"Afterward, I used to go to Tucson on horseback just to see her on weekends. That is if we were not playing for a dance that weekend. When we got married, I brought her to the ranch to live. I had already built a home for her. The ranch hands help to built it. That house still stands in Solomon today. A relative of the family lives there. Dolores, my wife gave birth to Cuca (Refugia), named after my mother (Refugia), Beatrice, Pablo, Ernesto, Rafael, Dolores, Alfredo, and Manuel. Manuelito died six months after being born, Dolores died also. All of your older brothers and sisters were born in Solomonville like me. I was born in Solomon. After the death of Dolores, I met your mother, Rita Soto Moreno. I met her also at a dance in Globe, Arizona. We were playing for the miners in Globe, Arizona. Your mother was born in a settlement called San Pedro. She went to live with her grandmother at the age of two in Reddington, Arizona. Your mother was very young when I met her. I married your mother about nine months after Dolores died. Rita raised Dolores's children. Your mother loved Dolores's children like they were her own. Rita in reality became Dolores's children's mother."

I found out on my research the truth of what really happened, why they had to leave the family property. This is what really happened. Tio Regino was going to go to prison for stealing some farm implements (not a steer), and was caught by the owner of the farm equipment, who pressed charges against him. Somebody made a deal with Regino about going along on this silent conspiracy to get the land of our grandfather after his death. The government found that gold was in that land and other precious minerals also. We found out through the Office of Senator John McCain of Arizona that the United States government put out a bid to dig that gold out of grandfather's land for their gain. They took out $22.5 million from the land. I, Ramon, found out in my research into our grandfather's homestead certificate how his family lost this land.

Let me say this here now. All the family really believed that the land did belong to Uncle Regino when they left the land and moved to the town of Solomonville. I will get back to that after I explain the story my father was telling me about Regino.

"Son, my Tio Regino got plenty of money on the land. He built a saloon bar in Solomon, that it still is there and being used by a white family who bought it from Tio Regino. When he had it build, he had some women of ill repute working out of the saloon. He had on the back of the building about eight tents with beds, wooden stoves, and chairs."

The women would work the saloon at night and take the men to their tents. If one of those women would run off with a cowboy, Tio Regino would go to Mexico and bring new ones to replace whoever he lost. This I say to my family. Remember that Tio Regino went to the ranch with some law marshals. The papers they delivered to grandmother were fraudulent papers. Tio Regino was in this conspiracy with Mr. and Mrs. Mashbir who had a land realty company. Later, her husband became a judge in Safford. But the land conspiracy started before that time. I get to that later on the history. I want to finish my father's story.

Chapter 13

Ramon hears his father, Pablo, speak about Blas Ortiz and how he remembers Blas and why. Blas was a farmhand working for Francisco. Blas Ortiz was also on the land conspiracy. He received the homestead certificate of Francisco's heirs and hid it for years, until his death in Tempe, Arizona.

These were his deep feelings concerning Blas Ortiz. "I learn to love him as my father after my father's death. Blas married my mother about a year after. This was in 1892. I don't know if they got married in Tucson or Solomon. Blas was a good husband to my mother and a good father to us. He looked at us as if we were his own. He never mistreated my mother and us. He took good care of us. Your Tia Carmen, Francisco, and myself. We learned to love him as our own father." I met Blas Ortiz. In the beginning all of Rita's children believed that he was really our grandfather because all my father's older children, even though they were already grown-up, used to call him grandfather. This is my personal account of Blas Ortiz. I got to know him when he and grandma Refugia came to live with us for a while. At this time, we no longer lived at the railroad section. We moved to 520 West 1st Street in Tempe. I remember Blas this way; I was but a small child about four years of age. He would take me in his lap and give me coffee with bread or whatever he was eating. This was every day that he gave me coffee. At that time, parents didn't know that coffee was bad for a young child.

Finally the coffee took its toll on me. I got so sick, that everybody thought that I was going to die. No, by some miracle, I got well, but from that day on, no more coffee. I also remember that grandpa Blas dug the ditch that ran from the Bertelsons home on West Roosevelt Street and West 1st Street to ours, which was about one block and a half. I remember seeing him come in to eat lunch wearing his big black hat and Indian leather boots to his knees. Blas and my father used to plant vegetables in a piece of ground next to an area close to the house. My father and brothers and sisters; they told me that Blas carried an Indian pouch on his belt and that he never let it away from him. We don't know what he had inside because he never took it off. This I found out later, as a matter

of fact, it was in 1994. But let me finish concerning Blas Ortiz. I haven't
found out who died first: grandmother or Blas. Anyway, Blas went fishing
at the Bertelson backyard because the canal ran behind the property of
the Bertelson house. There was a huge cottonwood tree and according
to the family, Blas would sit against the tree and do his fishing for catfish
and perch. One day he didn't come home and it got late. So Ralph, our
brother, went to the canal to see if he was there fishing. Ralph found Blas
dead. He was sitting down and had his back against the tree. He died of a
heart attack. When they took the body to the mortuary, they gave our father
the pouch and Blas's fishing tackle box. Father put those items away and
never looked into the pouch to see what was inside. This is an old Indian
custom, never look into anything that an ancestor left when he dies. Father
honored that custom. If he had opened the pouch, he would have been
surprised of what was inside of that pouch. As I go on the family history,
the mention of that pouch will again come into focus and the family will
be astonished of what Blas had inside of the pouch. My father loved Blas.
As far as he was concerned, Blas was his father. Blas took care of him at age
nine. The family loved Blas also because he took good care of them like he
was their real father. But Blas was the apple of his eyes. When father was
telling me about Blas, tears fell from his eyes, and he said to me, "I loved
him as a son loves his father."

That is why the family never mentioned our own grandfather, Francisco.
Blas had become the grandfather to all of father's older children. So
we, too, accepted Blas Ortiz as our grandfather. Even today, we all call
him grandfather and not plain Blas. As far as we feel about him. He was
our grandfather until I discovered what really happened that the family
lost their land in Solomon, Arizona. What our own father and our uncle
Francisco never knew was that when our grandfather went to Tucson to the
General Land Office (GLO) in 1890, he went to convert his preemption
land into an Indian Trust Patent. Grandfather Francisco did not know how
to read and write in the "English language." I was told by my father that
he never spoke in English, only in Indian language and very little Spanish.
When the recorder and receiver agent for the General Land Office in
Tucson attended to him, he had an interpreter to help him explain what
he wanted to be done on his land. Instead of providing grandfather with
the Indian land application, this individual gave him the wrong application
forms to fill out. This application forms were the normal land application
forms for all United States citizens and those that intended to become
citizens of the United States of America. "This was the law on filling for
homestead land."

This is where the silent conspiracy started. The federal government
knew what was in that land. They had already taken a survey of all the land

in that area and found large deposits of gold. The federal government contracted seven companies to dig the gold out of our grandfather's land. They took $22.5 million dollars worth. My brother Antonio (Tony) and I went to see Senator John McCain from Phoenix, Arizona, to see if he could help us get our land back. It was the senator that found that gold was discovered by the government surveyors in our grandfather's ranch. That is why the family was run off the ranch, to get that gold out.

Chapter 14

Ramon hears his father talk on his orchestra playing in the mining towns of Arizona, how they would travel in horse wagons to get to the town they were going to play. He talks on what went on when the miners got drunk with liquor and how the orchestra players would get some sleep.

Father started telling me about his early music playing. This is what he said about it. That when they got a contract to play at one of the towns, like Bisbee, Morenci, Miami, Clifton, this would be the copper miners in Miami or Morenci, they would load all their instruments in one horse wagon and all the musicians would go on another horse wagon. They would take plenty of water, food, and oats for the horses. Father played the violin, bass fiddle, and guitar. Pablito played the banjo, Ralph played the guitar, and Tio Pancho played the base fiddle and guitar. The other musicians played the trombone, saxophone, and trumpet. We would play for hours for the miners. They would make their parties for two or three days and nights. They would drink and eat, drink, drink, and pass out. When they woke up, they started drinking again. In order to get some rest and sleep, we would sneak one musician to go and sleep two hours, then we send another to do the same until we all had rested and slept. The miners never found out what was happening. Those miners and their families were a happy group of people. They had to be tough in order to survive the dirty work inside of the mines. The women did a lot of work in their homes. The women came from good stock. They were pioneers from the Midwest of the United States. Their parents fought in the Civil War, between the North and South. After the war, some of the people left the south and came west and fought our people. They called our people Indians, not Americans.

To them, our people were nothing but savages. Not all of our people like war. The peaceable Indians found work on the mines and work alongside Mexicans and whites. Venially they were accepted as Mexicans instead of Indians. Father laughs at this. He said to me, "Funny what a haircut does to a man. My mother used this saying. When we lived on the mountains, we were called Indians, but once we came down to the town and dressed as they dressed, we were called Mexicans. The mines were very hot inside, so long hair was cut and then they started calling you a Mexican because all our men look like the Mexicans. Most of them would say, I'm Mexican to be left alone. Mexicans at that time were treated better than the Indians. Hijo," he then said, "we were very happy in Solomon, especially living in town. Your brothers and sisters play around town. They use to play on the hanging gallows where they used to hang cattle and horse rustlers. At that time, if a person stole a horse or steer and got caught, they gave them trial, and if found guilty, they hanged them."

We happened to see two hangings in town. People used to come to town like they were coming to see a parade. They would dress up with their finest cloth; women would wear very pretty hats and long dresses. They would bring in the children and picnic food baskets and make it a day of enjoyment. People were glad to see the rustlers hanged. Some of them had lost horses and steers to men like those they hanged. Mothers and fathers used these hangings as a lesson to their children. That if you break the law by doing bad things to people and get caught and found guilty of such an act, they hang you for the crime committed. This part of the family history was told to me by my father at the Tempe Saint Luke Hospital after his hip operation. This was in August 1973. He was also operated for prostate problems. Little did I know that I was talking with my father for the last time he would be alive. I had spent two weeks visiting him at the hospital. I had taken two weeks of vacation from my federal job to be with him. I left after seeing that he was getting well; also, my vacation days were over. So the family took off to California (San Diego). We had only been in San Diego for one week when they called to tell me that father had died of an infection. They told me that the tube he had to drain his water from his bladder was left too long and the skin started to grow around the plastic and when they yanked it out, he started to bleed and that was how the infection started.

Chapter 15

Ramon hears his father reveal his Indian ancestry and the killing of Gabrial Sainz by his father Jesus Sainz. Pablo Jr. gives an account of the history of Tempe when they came in the 1920s. Ramon has that transcript that his brother wrote for the Tempe Historical Museum.

I will always cherish my last days spent with my father. This is because it was the first time that my father treated me as a son. I mean he really showed me his love to me. Father was always stricter with me than with his other children. I will tell my family how I was mistreated by him for telling the truth to things that I saw and told him about; how he would beat me up with a horse whip, belt buckle, or anything he could get a hold of. But for now, it was a very close feeling we felt for each other. He would hug me, kiss me on the cheek, put his hand on my head or shoulder. Maybe he was telling me how sorry he was for treating me the way that he did when I was a teenager. I feel that that was his way of saying "I'm sorry son for the ways that I treated you, please forgive me." It took me quite a few years to forgive my father. But I finally realized that in order for me to have peace of mind and not to be tormented by those horrible dreams that I had of his abuse, I had to forgive him. I forgave him and I have been in peace within me since then.

Now getting back to the story of the family. Our father had never said anything about us being Indians. That is, full-blooded Indians. His second sons, Rita's children, we, knew we had some Indian in us because our mother was Pinaleno Indian. The genealogy in the beginning of the history of the family was found by me (Ramon) before father told me the Indian part of our history. Now these are his exact words; how he told me his Indian background. "Son, your grandfather and grandmother were Apache Indians. (He's talking about his father Francisco and his mother Refugia.) My father was born in Ojo Caliente (Warm Springs), New Mexico, and my mother was born in Las Cruces, New Mexico.

My father was a Warm Springs Apache and my mother was a Mescalero Apache from Las Cruces. (Please note that Ojo Caliente is located in Taos County, New Mexico.) After they got married, they lived in Las Cruces until your Tia Carmen was born, then they came to live in Solomonville.

It was in Solomonville, that your uncle Francisco and I were born. Your mother, Rita, was also an Apache. She was born inside of the San Carlos Apache Reservation in a section of the reservation called San Pedro. Rita, your mother, was taken to Reddington to live with her grandmother at the age of two." Then he looked at me and smiled, and said to me, "I'm also Apache Indian son."

This is when I asked father, "Why didn't you tell us this when we were growing up?"

He responded, "At this time there was still a lot of anger concerning the Indian people in Arizona. If the State would have found out that all of you were Indians, they would have taken you and your brothers and sisters to live at the boarding school on Indian School Road, known as Phoenix Indian School. We heard stories that Indian children were sexually abused by the priests and nuns there. That they would whip them like animals and tell them that they were nothing but savages. Some of those children disappeared from school and were never heard of again. I didn't want this to happen to any of you, so I kept quite, so did Carmen and Francisco. People in Tempe figured that we were Mexican American. So that's the way we lived as Mexicans. Your mother had the tendency to talk Apache now and then. I had to tell her not to do it or else people would find out that we were Indians. I figured this out; if they thought we were Mexican American, none of us would have to suffer under the white people. The Indians were treated like animals. Our people suffered all kinds of injustices. Also, we wanted the best education we could give all of you to learn like the white man children. Indians were not properly educated like the white men."

Deep inside me, I have always been proud of my father's and mother's Indian ancestry. Then he said to me, "Son, be proud of what you are and never tarnish the name Chavarria." Its an Indian name, I found this out when I was researching family records. The name came from our people. The name is pronounced Echeverriah (Ahwanchevari) Juan Chavari. Later in the 1800, it was spelled *Cheverriah*. My father could only remember that the government had changed the name because they could not pronounce it. Father told me that if I hadn't asked concerning the family history, he would have kept quiet until his death. I felt that I was blessed in him telling me all that I'm writing in my family history. After I write the Tempe history of my brother Pablo (Paul) the one he wrote for the Tempe Museum. He starts his history this way:

> This history is written by Paul Amado Chavarria (Pablo). He was born 10/25/09, Solomonville, Arizona, son of Pablo Montoya Chavarria and Dolores Amado Chavarria. His mother was born 1885 in Altan, Sonora, Mexico. Dolores was Jewish Mexican. Pablo

Sr. was born in 1882 in Solomonville, Arizona. His occupation was musician, railroad worker, (Arizona Eastern Pacific), and flour miller for Hayden Flour Mill in Tempe, Arizona. Here is Paul's account of their journey from Solomonville to Tempe. (Dolores Amado was the first wife of our father to accompany her family's move to Tempe in 1918. Dolores died in 1921, and Rita Moreno married our father, nine months after her death.)

Chapter 16

Ramon lets his brother Paul tell about Tempe, of what he remembers of it. Paul tells how they came to live at the Casa Viega. Paul did not know that his grandfather had stayed overnight at the same place when he came over to see if he could talk to Geronimo's warriors to go back to the reservation.

My Memories of Tempe

Arriving in Tempe in 1918 when I was 19 years old, I saw a small town. Mill Avenue extended from 1st Street to Southern, where it ended. All streets were dirt narrow roads. The cement sidewalks were one foot higher than the streets. Hitching posts were used. Horses and wagons were the only transportation available. Few cars were in existence. The law consisted of one Constable—Smith, who had a horse patrolling the area. Tempe had a curfew ordinance. A bell placed at the old Tempe City Hall, was rung at 9 p.m. Children who were on the streets at that hour ran home like jack rabbits, for if the Constable caught up with us, he threatened to put us in jail. The bell was also used as a fire alarm. "The Casa Viega" had an upstairs, but was remodeled and made into apartments. This is where we lived in 1923. "Many Mexican families" lived there. The rest of the building was used as a grain storage area for the "Hayden Flower Mill," mice and scorpions were plentiful. The "Salt River" ran swiftly presenting a danger to all. But we had a swimming hole that was on the north side of the big "Butte." The second swimming hole was between the Tempe bridge and the railroad bridge. The first divers were the twins, John and Eddie Curry. They dove from the rails of the old bridge. The "Curry's" own the Tempe Hardware Store for many years. The upstairs of the building was used as a social hall. The "Mexican dances were held at the 'Midway Hall'" above the busy corner clothing store located where the Tempe Post Office is now located at 5th and Mill. In the early 1922, the Mexican families were entertained by a tent show. The owner of the show was a combined clown and comic named Jesperin. He had singers, acrobats, and dancers. Tickets for the show ranged from 25c to 50c per performance. My father, Pablo M. Chavarria, his brother Francisco (Frank) and a compadre, Eluterio Ballesteros, provided the music for the presentations.

The show was presented around the valley in 1918. My brother Ralph and sisters Betty C. Castro, Cuca Chavarria, and I attended the old 8th Street Public School, located at the corner of Mill and University. My favorite teachers were Miss Mendora and Mrs. Hodnet, sisters to the twins John and Eddy Curry. Serving as a truant officer was "Cresencio Cigala," father of Ray, Charlie, and Sofia. In 1923, my father, Pablo, was employed by the Arizona Eastern Railroad, which later became the Southern Pacific. At the age of 14, I too worked with my father as a substitute for the railroad. In 1926, the Hayden sisters, Betty and Sally, remodeled the Casa Viega Restaurant, now known as Monties. At a later date, a patio was opened and used to serve clientele. Mexican food was served; no beer or liquor was sold due to the probation era. Music was provided by Pablo Chavarria Sr. orchestra. My father played the violin; Pablo (Paul Jr.) played the guitar; Jesus Arroyo, the trumpet; Gabriel Caravajal, trombone; Jose Maria Arroyo, bass; Baldemar Caravajal, clarinet. The vocalists were Paula Luque and Matilda Acedo; their favorite song was "Una Noche Serena Y Oscura."

I remember my twelve-year-old brother Ralph Chavarria serenading the customers, playing his violin. He worked on weekends earning 50 cents per night plus tips. Betty Chavarria Castro and Cuca Chavarria waited on tables. They earned 50 cents per evening and tips. I met Audelia Guerra, the daughter of Don Benino y Doña Lazara Guerra. We were married three years later at the old Mount Carmel Catholic Church, located at the corner of College Ave. and Eighth Street (now known as University Dr.). We have two children, Pablo (Paul) Guerra Chavarria Jr. III and daughter Lillian Chavarria Krois. We lived at the Casa Viega upstairs, facing Mill Ave.

In December 1941, I started working for the Hayden Flower Mill where I worked for forty (40) years. My coworkers were Manuel Peralta, Juan Lopez, Lucio Lopez, Wally Acedo, Joe Cons, Geraldo Peralta. As the years passed by, we were able to witness the growth that took place at the Flower Mill. Our barrios no longer existed due to the growth of our city. The changes that have taken place as the years have passed on have been for the best. After the death of my wife "Audelia," my health started to fail me.

Josie Ortega Sanchez, a close friend of the Chavarria family, offered to take care of our brother Paul at her own home. Before his death, Paul gave my brother Tony, who lived close to him, some family history. Later, Paul related to me some more history of his youth and all his brothers and sisters when they were small; how they played together in Solomonville, Arizona. He said to me, "Monchie, we played around the hang man's platform. This is where they hanged the cattle and horse thief." Then I said to my brother Paul, "Some of our brothers and sisters told me the same thing about you and them playing in town. They all laughed at what you guys and girls did, when you played together." My brother Paul was still alive when I started to write our family history. He passed away nine months later. He had cancer of the bone (leukemia). This happened in 1995, a few months after I had started on the family history. I loved my brother Paul; he always demonstrated his love to all of us. Paul always provided me with counsel when I ask for some advice when I was growing up. I pray that Heavenly Father will bless him with the highest blessings in Heaven of Eternal Marriage to his devoted wife and companion, Audelia, whom he loved deeply.

Josie Ortega Sanchez provided me with this extra information on my brother Paul. Josie took good care of Paul on his last days here on earth.

Josie Ortega Sanchez was the person who wrote my brother's "Memories of Tempe". Paul told me that what he did was to tell Josie what he remembered about his youth and the rest of his brothers and sisters and Josie wrote it down for him. Paul was getting very ill at that time and he didn't have the strength to write. So Josie wrote for him. As we know by now that our father, Pablo Sr., brought his family to Tempe in 1918. This was his first family with Dolores Amado. After her death in 1921, this is when father met my mother, Rita, and married her. We figured that father married my mother nine months after Dolores's death because he needed a woman to take care of his children. Remember that Cuca (Refugia) was the oldest of the children. Cuca was just fifteen years of age and she couldn't take care of so many little ones.

I don't know if my father married my mother because of that or he fell in love with her because my mother Rita was Indian. Dolores Amado was Mexican Jewish. In pictures that I have seen of both Dolores and Rita, both women were very pretty and had nice bodies. Dolores must have weighted 112 pounds and Rita, my mother, about 120 pounds. According to the family, both women were very hard workers. They were excellent cooks and they did all their clothes by hand. Both were very helpful with the neighbors during their marriages to my father. My mother, Rita, was a guitar player. Mother and father would play together at home. Mother was also a singer, not only did she play the guitar, but she also sang with dad playing his violin. I never hear her play. I was too little when she died; my older brothers hear her play and sing. Mother also knew the Apache language and taught Rudolpho (Fito) how to speak it. Rudy, as I call him, used the Apache language at the San Carlos Apache Reservation when he worked for the Hayden Flower Mill in Tempe as a delivery truck driver for the mill. Now I'll get back to Paul's history again. My mother, Rita, came to Tempe in 1923 with father's first family by Dolores Amado. Paul was fourteen years of age when they moved to Tempe and he found employment in the Arizona Eastern Railroad as a substitute rail worker. Paul developed an interest in playing the guitar. He learned playing the guitar with one of his cousins.

Chapter 17

In this chapter, Paul writes some of his history of what he remembers of Tempe including his playing music with our father Pablo Chavarria Sr. Josie Ortega Sanchez writes more of Paul's history. At this time, our brother Paul is getting sicker and is unable to write himself. Also in this chapter is a small part on Tio Pancho (Francisco), father's older brother.

Paul and Ralph played together for the first time in 1923 at a wedding reception. Paul was fourteen and Ralph was nine years of age. In reminiscing, they both enjoyed a good laugh, for they only knew two polkas and one waltz. They played this music scores over and over again for at least four hours. No one cared. They all just enjoyed dancing to the music. Paul started to play with his father and his orchestra that consisted of seven musicians. Serious problems faced the musicians: the lack of transportation. Very few people could afford cars at that time. Paul recalls that Mr. Jose Maria Arroyo had a 1924 Model T Ford, which they used for transportation. Six musicians placed their musical instruments in the car with them inside; it was kind of crowded. They traveled all over the towns in Arizona playing for dances and weddings and other functions, getting paid one dollar ($1) per hour per musician. Many times after they would be done playing, the borrachitos (drunks) would hire them to play to their sweethearts for an hour or two. Sometimes they played till the wee hours of the morning. They would arrived in Tempe around seven or eight in the morning and sleep all day.

The law changed this tradition and it is no longer allowed. During the depression in 1937, Paul and his father joined the WPA string orchestra until 1940. The program was terminated then. They practiced on Mondays through Fridays and were paid $45 per two weeks work playing. The musicians were considered skill labors. In 1940, a group was organized called "LOS RANCHERITOS." Members consisted of Pablo Sr., Pablo Jr., Mike and Ben Gamboa. They played at baptisms, birthdays, weddings, etc. In 1927, Paul was called to join a group of musicians from Guadalupe. Mike Lopez was the group leader until they disbanded in 1931. In 1932, Paul married Audelia Guerra, daughter of Benino and Lazara Guerra, old timers from Tempe. Paul and his wife had two children, Paul III is a retired school principal and daughter Lillian Krois lives in Seattle, Washington. Paul recalls with humor, his father buying him a banjo guitar, when he was eighteen years of age.

Every time it rained, the skin on the banjo damped the strings and would become loose. He had to look for a stove to dry the skin in order to continue playing. Paul worked for forty years at the Hayden Flower Mill until his retirement. He and his brother Ralph joined Mike and Ben Gamboa volunteering many hours entertaining the senior citizens at the Escalante Senior Center. The Fiestas Patias at the center were magnificent because of the music provided by these Tempe musicians, bringing songs of long ago. Paul recalls the happiest moment of his life, when he got married and the day his son joined his musical group at the age of twelve by playing the trumpet. Paul beams with pride as he says of his son, "He was great." (I, Ramon, personally want to thank Josie Ortega Sanchez in providing this part of our brother Paul's history. Josie and her family have been close friends for many years. We all attended school together. I played football, softball, basketball with Charlie Ortega, her younger brother, and Rudolpho [Fito] played with Louis Ortega. This was in 1934 to 1943 at the Tempe Grammar School, Tempe, Arizona. Josie took care of our brother Paul in her home. When Paul passed away into the spirit world, Josie was in his bedside until his last breath. Josie and her family are part of the Chavarria's history. Friends like Josie don't come easy. She is still alive and resides in Tempe, Arizona. Yet in her years, she remains our friend. All I can say to you Josie is this, if and when your time comes to leave this earth, may you rest in the kingdom of Almighty God forever and even worlds without end. Amen.)

Now I give an account of Uncle Francisco, our father's brother. Tio Pancho, as we all call him, was born in Solomonville, Arizona, on September 13, 1880. He was two years older than our father, Pablo. He was also a musician; he played the guitar. Uncle Frank was grandfather's second child. Grandfather named him after him, "Francisco." His first wife was Ysenta Alderete. After her death, he married Isabel Peralta. Uncle Frank's first wife gave birth to three children namely Federico (Lico), Roberto (Beto), and Virginia. Uncle Frank's second wife gave birth to three children: Oscar, Ramon, and Juan. Tio Pancho was a very quiet person, most of the time he spend his time alone or with his family. He did not associate himself with other people. He wasn't the type to go visiting people at their homes. He took after his father, our grandfather, Francisco. He worked the family fields in Solomonville. After the family lost the ranch in 1904, he went to work at the mining company of Phelps Dodge in Morenci, Arizona. Later in the late 1930, he moved with his family to Phoenix, Arizona. When he moved to Phoenix, he used to play with my father on occasions. He was a very good guitar player, but didn't like to play all the time.

Uncle Frank and my father played together at Tio's house. Pablo's family would visit his brother's family in Phoenix and stay all day. Both brothers used to play together all afternoon. They both would laugh about some of the music they were playing.

Uncle Frank liked to play at weddings parties. This is where he would see his old friends from different parts of Arizona. When he lived in Phoenix, my father would go visit him and I would tag along. I love playing with my cousins Ramon and Juanito. Father and uncle would get together, talk, and have a few cold beers and start playing all the music they knew. This went on for hours, during this time I played with Ramon and Juanito.

Chapter 18

Ramon is mistaken for his cousin Ramon, son of Francisco Chavarria. Here I am going to talk about how his uncle Francisco died and about his cousin's mental institution years of being away from the family.

Tia Isabel always fed us before going home. She enjoyed cooking for us. She had a talent for cooking. We never left her home without her feeding us. One of the memories that I will always remember is this, Ramon, my cousin had a habit of walking backward. He would meet you face to face and when he met you and went passed you talking to you, he would turn around and walk backward still talking to you. This habit got him into trouble with people that he didn't know. Someone must have reported him as being crazy because somebody turned him in to the Phoenix police as being crazy and they put him in the mental disturbed hospital on 24th and Van Buren streets in Phoenix. I went to see my cousin Ramon at the hospital several times while he was there. Ramon would ask me, "Monchie, why am I here in this hospital? This place is for crazy people and I'm not crazy like them." I would answer him and say, "Primo (cousin), I don't have the answer. Your family should know why you are in here."

To this day, I really don't know why he was admitted and why the family didn't try to get him out. He did tell me that he was treated very well in the hospital. He had nice clothes, good food, and all the sex he wanted with the young girls that were admitted in there. Ramon stayed in the hospital for five years. The family had already moved to Tucson when Ramon got out, the last time that I heard from one of his uncles on his father's side. Cousin Francisco lives in Sierra Vista, Arizona, about sixty miles from Tucson. He told me that Ramon married and had two boys and one girl from his marriage; that cousin Ramon had died two years ago (2001 in Tucson) and is buried there. His children all got married and have children of their own and they all reside in Tucson. Cousin Francisco also told me that Ramon's wife is still living in Tucson, Arizona, but is very ill.

The people in Tempe didn't know that we had two Ramon's in the family. They used to confuse me with Ramon, son of Francisco Chavarria, my father's brother. They would stop and ask me, what are you doing out of the crazy house. I would answer, "That's my cousin Ramon, son of my

Tio Pancho. I'm Ramon, son of Pablo Chavarria." Yet some did not believe me. They just shake their heads and went on their way. I could see it in their faces that they were still confused. The last time I saw my Tio Pancho was in the year 1940, just before the war with Japan in 1941. He moved again to Morenci, Arizona, to work on the copper mine there. The rest of the family and Uncle Frank (Pancho) came to see my father in that year; that I saw him for the last time. Tio Pancho was already ill with mining dust in the lungs. He would cough and spit blood out of his mouth. He told dad that his days were numbered on this earth.

This illness is caused by breathing sulfur without mask respirators. At that time, they didn't have the safety equipment they have today or the safety laws to protect the miner's underground work. This disease eats your lungs little by little until you die from it. It is a horrible sickness to get. One will never live once you get it. Tia Isabel died before Tio Pancho. She died in Tucson and is buried there. This is why Tio Pancho moved to Morenci, to work on the mine again and there is where he died. My father attended his funeral and it was him that filled out his brother's death certificate, my father believed that his brother's death was caused by his heavy drinking and the mine dust. Tio Pancho drank hard liquor like Great-Uncle Regino, even took it to work on his coffee thermal. He must have been an alcoholic if he had to drink every day. Tio Regino died as an alcoholic also.

Chapter 19

Ramon's father tells him why he doesn't drink hard liquor; that alcoholism runs in the Chavarria family. That is the way his uncle Regino died and his brother Francisco.

My father said to me, "Alcoholism runs in the Chavarria family. That is why I don't drink hard liquor. I drink one or two beers, and that's it. I personally don't remember our father drinking hard liquor. I saw him drink one beer or two and that was it." One very important part of our family history is this. This is the account of our grandfather Francisco after they had shot his father, 'Francisco, the butcher' at Fort Goodwin by the U.S. Cavalry. Remember that after the death of his father, our grandfather rode with Chief Cochise as a warrior. He did this because he was upset with the white eyes of the way they shot his own father like an animal. How many white eye he personally killed, we will never know, but he did kill many, not only did he kill white eyes, also Mexicans. Indians did not like Mexicans, though the Mexican is also of the Indian race. It was their evil ways of living. They liked to kill and steal from their own. They're liars, cheats, dirty, filthy, whore mongers, and adulators. The Indians of North America only killed when their lives or the families were in danger and had clean morals and respect for their wives and families.

Their plunders were only for food and utensils for cooking. As the white man came to their lands to plunder and rape their women, they learned from them how to scalp their enemies and to take captives as slaves. The Indians learn evil ways from the white men. Not the whites from the Indians. This I learned from my father. That the white man wrote their books to sell. They wrote a lot of lies about the Indians in order to sell the books and newspapers. That is the truth of what my father told me. You look at the history channel today and they are showing the true picture of what really did happen to the Indians in the 1700 and 1800. I don't pay much attention of all the stories about Indians. As of today, the American Indian is still in reservations. Nothing has changed in all this years. We are not free people in this "nation." Sooner or later, we will leave the reservations and take our rightful places in the American society. Then we will shout, "Free at last, free at last, thank God almighty, free at last." I took this saying from the late Dr. Luther King Jr. when he gave that historical White House speech at our National Capital.

My father said, "Son, your Tio Regino became an alcoholic simply because his father was killed by the white man. He couldn't forget how he was shot being shackled on his feet and hands. Tio Trinidad never said anything about the shooting of his father. What he felt inside is a different story. He didn't take any guff from the white man. He stood his ground and wasn't afraid of them." Tio Trinidad eventually moved to New Mexico to the Mescalero Indian Reservation and died there. He is listed in their Indian roll books at the reservation as living there. Tio Regino is buried in Solomon, Arizona. Most of his family is buried there. I visited their graves in 1994 with my little brother, Tony, and we took some video pictures of the land and the family cemetery plots.

Chapter 20

In this chapter, Ramon talks of his sisters' background of what he learns from them and also what he saw in them, their marriages and lives with their husbands, and what he saw and admired in each one.

Now I will give an account of my older sisters. What I will be stating are facts as I have seen them, including some of own personal stories before I was born. I will start with the oldest, which is Refugia (Cuca). Cuca was about twenty-one when I was born in 1927. I write their history not to degrade any of them. I write with all my love concerning them. I grow to love them very much. They were a lot of fun to be with. Not perfect, this is done in a manner as to show our future generation of the Chavarria's that we were not born perfect—that we also made mistakes in our lives, but we overcame them and each one of us grow in knowledge as we grew in age. What I can remember about Cuca is that she was and still is a very beautiful woman at age 94. One will never see her without her makeup. That is her first duty of the day, to put her makeup and get dressed before eating breakfast. This is a ritual every day.

She says that a lady always looks her best and acts like a lady at all times. Cuca, as I recall, moved from Tempe in the late thirties. She moved to Los Angeles, California, found work, and rented an apartment close to town. She told the family that she went out with movie stars. She had pictures of them with her at their homes. They treated her with respect and had a lot of fun dining and dancing with her. She had been in Los Angeles for a couple of years. She met Nick Ramirez, a professional boxer, and they got married. Cuca continued to work and Nick continued to box professionally. I personally met Nick in 1947. I was inducted into the armed forces and reported to Fort MacArthur in San Pedro, California. I was waiting shipping orders to go to Harlingen, Texas, for gunnery training on the B-29 bomber. Nick was a very handsome man. He didn't have any cuts on his face from boxing. He was a very kindhearted person. He took me all around Los Angeles. One Saturday before shipping out, they gave us a one-day pass to go to town. When I arrived at my sisters apartment, my sister Cuca opened the door to let me in and as I walked in I noticed that Nick had a teaspoon over the flame on one of the burners on the stove. Cuca noticed that I saw him and then she told me that Nick was addicted to cocaine. Nick looked at me and said "I'm sorry, that you saw this Monchie. I can't do without these injections." I do recall that I told him, "Nick you're my sister's husband. What you do in your home is your business, but if you don't leave it, this drug will send you to the grave." Cuca told me that Nick started to sell her clothes in order to get drug money for his habit. Nick was a tremendous boxer. How he got involved in drugs I don't know. Nick died of an overdose at a very young age. He was thirty-two when he died. Cuca never remarried. Cuca found work with an elderly Japanese gardener who did the landscaping for movies stars in Hollywood. If I can remember, his name was Tunie. My wife and I met him in 1949 in Los Angeles, California, when we went to Los Angeles to see if I could get a job painting automobiles. I had just graduated from vocational school at Thunderbird Field in Scottsdale, Arizona. I took training under the GI Bill after getting out of the air force in January 8, 1947. The course that I took was Body and Fender and Auto painting for two years. We stayed with Alfredo, my brother, and Ester, his wife, for six months. I never found work there, so we came back to Tempe, Arizona, and stayed with my wife's parents. We found a house for rent next to them and I went to work for the same company that I worked before going to California. As I mentioned before, Cuca moved to Scottsdale, Arizona. She found an apartment next to my other sister Betty. Cuca passed away in 1997 in Scottsdale, Arizona, and is buried there. As I can remember, this meeting with all of my sisters came by accident. I happened to take my wife to visit Betty and Cuca in Scottsdale in one of our trips to Arizona. We went to visit them and to our surprise, Lolita was also visiting my sisters. She had just gotten in from Gilroy, California, that morning. As the day passed by, the girls started telling my wife the history of the family when they lived in Solomon, Arizona. All of them including my older brothers were born in Solomon, Arizona.

My sister Betty started to show my wife (Margaret) pictures of their mother Dolores and the rest of the family. They have always enjoyed the company of Margaret. She has always been their favorite sister-in-law. I happened to have my recorder and I taped their conversation with my wife. They revealed to Margaret some of their dark secrets. As I continue writing our family history, some of the dark secrets will come to light, as our history starts to unroll into the past. This is what they remember about our older brothers, from our father's first marriage to Dolores Amado Chavarria. Pablo, whom we call (Pablito), was born very handsome. As he grew to manhood, Pablito started to play with my father's band. Pablito learn to play the banjo from one of our cousins who also were musicians. My sisters laughed as they told Margaret that the girls didn't leave him alone.

They made all kinds of flirtatious looks at him. Even married women would flirt with him as they danced with their husbands. The husbands would get jealous of Pablito and try to beat him up. Pablito was quite a ladies' man. He had this problem throughout his life. This weakness he had with women came to end. Pablito got married to Audelia Guerra of Tempe. She didn't put up with his habit of women, Lolie, as we call her, finally divorced Pablito. After their divorce, both started dating others. They never married others they went out with. They were single for five years. Lolie kept the two children they had, namely Paul III and Lillian. I personally had a talk with both of them separately. I saw that each cared for the other and loved each other, too. I was able to bring them together for a meeting at our father's house; our father had a long talk with both of them, especially with Pablito. Father let his son Pablito know how he felt about his no good habit of messing around with other women when he was already married and had two children.

Chapter 21

Pablito is reprimanded by his father Pablo Sr. of his behavior. Ramon also talks with both of them concerning their love toward each other. Both decide to remarry again and live a better life as a family.

Then came my turn to talk with each one separately. I asked each one their true feelings toward each other, about their children's future, their loyalty toward each other. And finally I asked them each one this question, "Pablito, do you love Audelia?" Pablito looked at her and said, "Yes, I do, very much and I'm sorry for all the hurt I have caused her to go through. I promise you that if she gives me another chance. She will always come first in my life and the children." Then I asked Audelia the same question. She responded, "Yes, I have always loved Pablo and still do very much." Then I said to both of them, "I'm going to leave both of you alone to talk things over without any interference from our father and I." When both came into the house about half an hour later, Pablito looked at me with a smile, looked at our father and said to him, "We are getting together again, Father. I have been very foolish in doing the things that I have done in the past. I will never again disgrace this family or Audelia. I will always love Audelia more than anything in my life. I will always have her on my side as a wife should be. She will never have to worry about me going back to my old habits again." My brother Paul (Pablito) never went back on his promise. Lolie, as we all call her, never had any trouble with our brother again. Paul stayed with her for the remainder of her life. Paul even went as far as quitting his music playing. Our brother was at Lolie's bedside when she passed away. Paul never married again.

Pablito remained faithful to her and cleaved to her with all of his heart. I bear my testimony that I know that Pablito and Audelia (Lolie) are together in paradise. This is the place where we all go after death to wait for the resurrection—the uniting of the spiritual body with the mortal body never again to taste death. This is the place also where we all will meet Father Adam and Mother Eve down to the present time.

Worlds without end. To my brother and Lolie, may the Lord God bless you both with the blessings that both of you earned here on earth. I love both of you. I will see you again never to be separated again by death.

Chapter 22

Ramon tells what he remembers about his brother Ernesto. Ernesto was the brother who took care of Ramon as a little boy until his death of typhoid fever. Ramon tells all that he did with his big brother Ernesto.

Now I write the history as I can remember of my dear brother Ernesto. Ernesto died at the age of twenty-seven as I can best recall. He died of typhoid fever in 1934, three years before my mother, Rita, died. Ernesto was a farm worker. He knew the work on a farm since he grew up in Solomonville. Grandmother Refugia was still living on the land that her husband left after his death in 1891. All of the Chavarria's have worked in the farm fields of agriculture at one time or the other, including my own children, "picking cotton." One hot summer day as Ernesto worked on the farm of Mr. Dobson on the outskirts of the city of Tempe, Arizona, Ernesto put a watermelon to cool off in the canal that ran in the center of Mr. Dobson's ranch. After he was done working, he decided to go swimming in the canal. My sisters told me that our brother Ernesto ate the watermelon. It turns out that after swimming, he got out to rest under a cottonwood tree next to the canal to rest and eat the center of the watermelon. It was the watermelon that he put in the canal to get cold that had the typhoid virus, and Ernesto came down with the virus.

When he started to get sick, our brother Roberto was already sick with the typhoid illness. Our brother took the responsibility to take care of Roberto. Ernesto stayed in the same room with Roberto taking care of him and all this time Ernesto never told anyone in the family that he had the virus too. He died after Roberto got well. Roberto for a year blamed himself for the death of Ernesto. It was the doctor that discovered the real reason for Ernesto's death. I have always admired my brother Ernesto. Why? Let me tell you what I personally remember about him. When I was seven years of age, he used to wake me up in the morning. He would take me out in the backyard of the house where the water faucet was. He would wash my face, ears, neck, comb my hair, dry me well, then he would swing me over his shoulders and run with me like as if he was a horse and made the noise of a horse. Oh, how I loved that! After playing with me, he would take me by the hand into the house and there he would cook me breakfast, oatmeal and scrambled eggs. He would also do my lunch for school. I was in the kindergarten at the Tempe Grammar School on Tenth Street. Ernesto was a very helpful person with people, especially in the railroad section where we lived. This railroad community consisted of families of the Railroad workers. This area was near the railroad tracks on Eighth and farmers, right on the corner. Today, this same area is a business district. They have changed the name of the street from Eighth Street to Tempe University Street and the railroad section is gone. I remember that Ernesto, not my mother, bought me a red tricycle. I really loved the red tricycle. I would hurry home just to ride it all over our backyard. I found a wooden screw and put it in my mouth, and continued to ride my tricycle. I found a board and I carried it to a tree stump and made a slide to ride my tricycle up that ramp. I remember what happened. I tried to ride my bike up the ramp to the top, but the bike front wheel went up and I slide off the bike and swallowed the screw. I started to cry and mom and Ernesto heard me, and they came running to help me. I told them that I had swollen a wooden screw that I had found and put it in my mouth.

My mother ran inside of the house and had a bottle of castor oil in her hand and made me drink what was left inside the bottle. It was a short time before I had a bowel movement and the screw and the wooden screw came out without causing any damage to my insides. I was lucky. It could have caused great damage inside my stomach intestines. Good thing that the screw went straight in and out. I could have had the screw gone sideways and gotten stuck inside my stomach and would have had surgery to remove it. My mother and Ernesto were very worried that the wooden screw would damage my intestines inside. All I can say is that the Lord God was taking care of me since my youth.

This I found out after I accepted him as my Savior and became a member of his church later on as a grown man. I received a blessing that he had and has been my protector since my youth. Mother saved the wooden screw for years and when she died, my father kept it until he died. The last time I saw that wooden screw was in 1955. I went over to visit my father and borrowed the birth certificates of all my brothers and sisters. It was at that time I had been baptized into the Church of Jesus Christ of Latter-day Saints, better known as the Mormon Church. This was in November 1954. Our father had all of his important documents in a fishing tackle metal box that was at one time his stepfather Blas Ortiz's, who had married his mother after the death of his father, Francisco Chavarria.

Father kept this metal box under lock and key. He didn't want his papers and documents stolen by anyone. I remember that father took all the papers and documents out of the metal box and laid them in front of me and told me, "Son, go through all the documents and take what you need for your research and then bring them back to me." I said to my father, "As soon as I am done with them, I will bring them to you as I promised I would." I was looking for the birth certificates of all my older brothers and sisters. I was getting ready to start my family genealogy (family history). When I selected the necessary documents, Father asks me that he wanted to see if I had everything that I asked for. He then said, "You need two more in here," and he opened an envelope and handed me his birth certificate and my mother Rita's death certificate. I was twenty-eight years of age at this time and living in San Diego, California. I saw every piece of papers and documents inside of that box. The reason that I'm stating this is because later on in the history of my little brother Antonio (Tony), he claims to have found a very important document inside of this box. If this document had been inside of that box, I would had seen it and also remembered the document or I would have asked father about it. In the history of my brother Tony, this will be coming out; how he found that document and still has it in the possession of his family.

Chapter 23

In this chapter, Ramon's sisters reveal the history of Ernesto. In his youth and later years, Ramon learns from his older sisters why Ernesto took care of him as a little boy.

This is how I came in possession of Ernesto's birth certificate and the rest of my brothers and sisters. When I saw Ernesto's birth certificate, I asked my father what really happened to Ernesto. He told me what happened to Ernest and what caused his death so young. In 1995, my wife (Margaret) and I went to Arizona on vacation. We went to Scottsdale to visit Betty and Cuca, who was living next to Betty in the same apartment complex. When we arrived at Betty's apartment, not only did we find Cuca there, but also Lolita, who had arrived there a few days ahead of us from Gilroy, California. We started on family history and I told them what I had been doing, in family research to trace our lineage roots. I told them what I remembered about Ernesto, that he has always been on my mind. That I can still see him carrying me on his back. That I know that when my time comes to an end here on this earth, I will see him again where he is now and the rest of the family. I told them, when I see Ernesto, I want to give him a good report of what I did on this earth.

I have always loved that brother with all my heart and still do. He loved me and took good care of me always as a young child. During our family conversations in different parts of the family history, Betty took out her photograph books to show Margaret pictures of the family. She had pictures of all of us. This is when I really saw my brother Ernesto, how he looked at the age of seventeen. At this time, Betty, Cuca, and Lolita said to Margaret, "Take a good look at Ernesto's picture, notice that Ramon is the living image of our brother Ernesto and have the same body structure that he had when he was your age at seventeen." At this time, Cuca (Refugia) said to all of us, "Ernesto was in the same likeness and image of our grandfather, Francisco." Then she said to me, "Ramon, take a good look at Ernesto's picture. You take after him; you look as if his twin brother." Then Betty said, "This is why Ernesto took good care of you as a child. He might have sensed that you were going to take after him in looks and have the same body structure as him. Ramon," Betty said to me, "Ernest as a young teenager did a lot of physical exercises on our backyard. He built an exercise gym in the back of the house and did his exercises every day. He developed his own pull-up bars by getting two thick lead pipes and putting cement inside of two five-gallon buckets and the pipes in the middle of the buckets. After the cement dried, he had push-up bars of different weights and sizes. He also had pull-up bars to pull himself up and down. He didn't smoke or drink liquor. He kept himself in shape all of his life. Ernesto never used profanity on anyone." I also learned from my sisters that Ernesto was quite a fistfighter. Betty told me that one day a circus came to Tempe to entertain the residence of Phoenix, Mesa, and Chandler at Tempe. She said that everyone had a lot of fun. "Ramon," she said, "let me tell you what happened at the circus. The circus had a prizefighter, and anyone that could stay in the boxing ring with him for three minutes would win twenty-five dollars. The boys that our brother hang around with coaxed him into getting in the ring with the circus fighter. He didn't want to at first, but the boys started to tease him of being afraid. Ernesto took his shirt off and climbed into the ring to fight. The fighter was much older than Ernesto. I would say about five years older. The fighter began to tease our brother, telling him to go to Mama. "You're nothing but Mama's little boy." Our brother looked at him and said, "Are you going to talk all night or fight?" This got the circus fighter all upset, and he came at Ernesto like a raging bull, ready to kill as Ernesto covered himself to protect his face and stomach. And out of nowhere, he stepped out to the right side of the fighter and threw two punches to the stomach of the fighter. The fighter bent in pain, and then Ernesto threw a right cross on the right side of the jaw and followed with a left hook to the chin, and the fighter went down on his back. He was completely knocked out.

Chapter 24

Ramon learns from his sisters that Ernesto was offered a job with the circus as a ring fighter. Ernesto beats up two Tempe bullies who later became our brother Pablito's brothers-in-law. One of these two tells Ramon what really happened.

The owner of the circus—after he saw what Ernesto did to his fighter—offered him the position as the circus fighter. Ernesto declined the offer. Our brother was not a violent person. He only defended himself from street bullies in town dances or if they picked on him wherever. Louis and Floyd Guerra were those kinds of person. They both tried to beat up Ernesto one day at the railroad section where we lived in Tempe. Both brothers went looking for Ernesto at our home at the railroad section where we lived. My sisters proudly said to both my wife and I, "Ernesto went out after hearing them yell for him to come out and see how good he was at fighting. He tried to reason with both of the Guerra brothers. They didn't want to listen to Ernest and both came at him. Our brother took both of the Guerra brothers on. When it was over, both brothers were on the ground flat-out. He gave them such a beating that they no longer bullied anyone else in Tempe. Louis, Floyd, and Benjamin (Benny) later became our brother Pablito's brothers-in-law when Pablo married their sister, Audelia Guerra.

I then related to my sisters, I know about that fight. When I was working at the Exchange Orange Product Company in Tempe, Floyd's wife was also employed there. Her name is Rebecca Sosa Guerra. Rebecca is still alive and living in Mesa, Arizona. On this day, her husband Floyd Guerra came over to take his wife home. Since he knew me as a little boy and later as a teenager, he struck a conversation with me. This conversation led to him telling me of the fight he and his brother Louis had with Ernesto. These are the exact words he used, "Your brother Ernesto was built like a brick wall. Every time I hit him, it was like hitting a brick wall. When he hit us, it seemed that his hands were made of rock. He tore me and my brother apart. We went home all bloodied. Our faces were a mess and our bodies ached like we had been hit by the train. We never again bullied anyone else again. Your brother told us that next time he heard that we ever tried to bully anyone else, that he would find us and give us the same treatment he had just given us." Floyd laughed and said, "Monchie, I can still feel his punches hitting me."

"So you see, Sis, I already knew about that fight when our brother beat up the Guerra brothers. Maybe this is why they treated our brother Pablo so good when he married their sister Lolie." They all started to laugh including me. All of these memories concerning our brother Ernesto will always be an important part of my life. I have always loved him as if he was still living today. I made a promise when I took Jesus Christ into my life as my Savior and Redeemer, that I would do all of his Temple Ordinances here on this earth, to have him sealed to our parents in the spirit world. This is my firm commitment to him to get all of these ordinances that we, as members of the Church of Jesus Christ of Latter-day Saints, are instructed by our Lord in the last chapter of the Old Testament of Malachi. I pray that our brother Ernesto is in the presence of all those faithful spirits that dwelled on the earth at one time or the other. I know that he is reunited with our departed family.

One very important part of my history is that after the death of Ernesto. I had no one to take care of me like he did. I started to go around with the children in our railroad section housing and getting into trouble one way or the other. One day, the older kids of the section lifted up the back wheels of the inspection cart. This cart was used to inspect the railroad tracks for damages. The cart was operated by pushing the front handles forward and backward. The cart had gears to make it move forward or backward with a shift handle. It also had two front wheels and a rear wheel. What the kids did was to raise the rear wheel and make it go, as if the cart was on the rails traveling. They would stop it by sticking rail spikes into the gears. I join them in this activity and when I stuck the spike into the gears, the spike flowed out of my hand and my fingers went into the gears and smashed my middle index finger. I remember yelling of pain and all the kids ran to their house before the parents found out what they were doing with the rail cart. I got a hold of my hand and ran home to my mother. Right away, she noticed that my middle finger was all broken up and bleeding terribly. They couldn't stop the bleeding, so they wrapped my hand with a towel and stuck my hand in a bucket with cooking flour. After they saw that the bleeding had stopped, they tried to remove the towel but the dried blood was caked dry and they couldn't remove the towel. What they did was they left that towel for a few days and then they stuck my hand in a pale of warm water to soak and they finally got the bandage off.

They never took me to a doctor or hospital and because of this negligence, I cannot bend the middle finger because it got fused to the index finger on my right hand today. I often wonder why I wasn't taken to a doctor to get it fixed or for medical attention. The family had money. We were not poor people. Even today, when I see my finger, it reminds me of my childhood when I went into the service of our country in the army air force in 1945. I hurt my finger in training and the medical doctors wanted to remove my middle finger. They told me that the finger was of no use to me, that I would always have trouble with it. I told the doctors that I wanted to keep my finger. Though my finger is fused together in the middle joint, I can still use it very well. I believe that I made the right decision in keeping it. It doesn't bother me one bit to use my right hand on anything that I do. I honestly believe that if my brother Ernesto had been alive when this happened, he would have done something, taken me to a doctor or hospital. As I write my history and the family, all this work in the temple has been accomplished for Ernesto and all my brothers and sisters. My father has been sealed to Dolores and my mother and my great-grandfather's also. The only ones left are my brother Ralph and his family. Roberto's family is going to do his temple work. Susan, his younger daughter, is a member of the church and has already been sealed to her husband and her own children. Now I will try to give an account of my brother Ralph, who is still alive and is in good health at age ninety. As I write some of this family history, the date is January 7, 2005, and at the moment, here in Las Vegas, our home. We are having a snow shower. It's very beautiful outside, all white.

Chapter 25

Ramon tells about his own knowledge of his brother Ralph and also his own personal view of his brother's life, his music, and his playing around the Sun Valley (Arizona) and San Diego, California.

Pablo Jr. (Pablito) gave me some very good information of our brother's life before he passed away. I thank him for all the information he gave me concerning all of the Chavarria family from Solomonville, Arizona. This was in the year 1992. Paul, as we used to call him, sometimes said to me, "Monie (He used to call me Monie instead of Monchie. Why? I don't know why.), to me Raphael has not been the easiest brother to get along with. All of us have learned not to argue with him too much." asked Paul why they try to avoid arguing with our brother Raphael.

. "Raphael has a temper if you get to argue with him on matters that he believes he's right and you're wrong. He has been this way since he was a little boy. He has never changed his ways; that's his character. If you don't get him upset, he will do anything to help you. One has to get on his good side." Paul laughed as he said this to me. "Once he makes up his mind, you can never change him one way or the other. He is plain stubborn in his own way. I don't judge our brother one bit. That's his character. One way or the other, he is still our brother and we love him so. Monie, we all have weaknesses and that happens to be his. Yes, we have had some good disagreements in our childhood as teenagers and grown-ups. But we always make up. We are brothers and we love each other."

This is how he started telling me about the background of Ralph's history. "He was our fathers' favorite because he started to become a good musician like our father. He never argued with father as I did and he always did what father told him to do even if he didn't like doing it. He started to play music at a very young age and began to play with our father's band. Even though, I also played with our father, Ralph was the apple of his eyes. He learned to play the violin like our father at an early age. Maybe father saw himself at that age that he was looking at Ralph. Maybe he saw himself trying real hard to become a good violin player. Ralph won the heart of our father at a young age until father died in 1973. Ralph was lost for a while after father's death. As a young musician, Ralph used to go with us to the mining camps around Bisbee, Morenci, Reddington, Clifton, Globe Miami, and Safford and around the towns of Arizona. Monie," he said to me, "Ralph at the age of twenty, he played as well as father and father felt so proud that he had a son that took after him in mastering the violin. Later in life, Ralph took to playing the bass fiddle."

"I believe he did this in order as not to give father any competition on the violin. That's my opinion, anyway. I was also proud of my brother the way he played the violin. Matter of fact, I'm still proud of him today. Ralph and I learned to play music by note from our father. Our father never would take anyone to play with his band unless he knew how to play by note. Our father never approve any musician that played by just hearing the music and playing by ear, not by note. Father believed that if you couldn't learn by note, you had no business playing music. He believed that if you knew music by note, that you can play with any band of professional musicians anywhere anytime. After our brother Ralph married Consuelo Huerta from Phoenix, Arizona, he formed his own orchestra in Phoenix with the best musicians he could find in the surrounding areas of Phoenix." Ralph and Pablito started playing after our father told them to go and play their own type of music. Ralph at this time had developed his talent of composing his own style of modern music. His orchestra played all over the state of Arizona.

His orchestra would pack them into the ballrooms, American legion halls, and veterans of foreign wars. His orchestra played top Latino music to perfection. Ralph's orchestra was considered the top Latino orchestra throughout the state of Arizona for seventeen years. Ralph's' orchestra also played in California. He played in San Diego, California, for the largest Hispanic National Organization of California, The American GI Forum of the United States of America. Twice he played in San Diego, once in Oceanside, California. I happened to move to California with my family in 1954 and lived in Chula Vista, California. I joined the GI Forum in 1961, and I happened to be an officer of the organization in San Diego and headed the entertainment committee of the GI Forum Chapter of San Diego. I recommended my brother's orchestra from Phoenix, Arizona. The name of the orchestra was called "Chapito Chavarria Band." Ralph had recorded some of his music on tapes and He gave me a set of six recordings for my own to keep.

I played the tapes to the entertainment committee and they all voted to hire my brother's orchestra to play for our state national convention that year in San Diego, California. I was very proud when they started to play that evening. Nobody wanted to sit down, they stayed on the dance floor waiting for the next dance. Members of the committee came to me and said, "If we don't do something right away, we are going to lose money on the percentage of the bar drinks. Nobody is buying drinks because they don't sit down and buy a beer or mix drink." I told them, "Let's go and talk with my brother and see how he can help us on this matter." Ralph was very cooperative on this matter. He suggested that he could take a little longer in playing the next number, so that the people would get tired of waiting and go sit down for a while and buy some drinks. He also suggested to take an extra ten minutes on their break. All this was approved on the spot and we did make our percentage on the bar drinks and more. Thanks to my brother's suggestions.

Everybody wanted more music after they had fulfilled their contract for the four hours of music. We passed the hat and received enough donations for another hour of dance music. Everyone there praised my brother and his band for the good music they played. The same evening after the dance, all the state officers of the GI Forum of the national organization gave my brother a contract to play again for the organization the following year in San Diego at our national convention to be held in San Diego, California. That also was a tremendous success. I was the most popular member of the organization due to the success of my brother's playing. Never again did San Diego have an orchestra so successful in bring the people in as my brother did. His orchestra, "Chapito Chavarria's Band," built such a reputation in Arizona that he had a contract with the Calderon Dance Hall for seventeen years to play Saturdays and Sundays. This was on Sixteenth Street and Buckeye Road, Phoenix, Arizona. He played there until the place had to be sold to the City of Phoenix to widen the road. My wife Margarita and I used to go dancing at Calderon's Ballroom to his music of mambos, cambias, pachangas, and waltzes. Ralph composed or rearranged the music they played. All of the Chavarria's family got to see the two brothers, Paul and Ralph, play with our father at their parties for years. Our father played his last music with Ralph and Paul at the age of ninety. Father died at the age of ninety-two.

Ralph taught his three sons music and the piano. He was like our father. First, he taught them the note scale, then the actual playing of the piano instrument. Two of his sons played with the orchestra at the Calderon Ballroom. Mike never took the music seriously. He became an auto mechanic of the Rolls-Royce Corporation in Phoenix. He plays the piano just for fun like Victor Borg, the piano comedian. Mike is good on the piano, but he prefers working on cars better. Ralphie plays with his church group, now that his father has retired from playing. He also plays with his father and his brother Ernie now and then. Ernie has a music studio in Mesa, Arizona. He also teaches music by note scale. Both brothers have traveled around the world playing in concerts. Now that they are older, they play at home. They get calls to go play at universities around Arizona.

They are very good musicians. World-renowned, both of them. Ralph Sr. also had a daughter named Barbara. She didn't want to play music. She has worked for the Phoenix National Bank for a great number of years. Our brother Paul remained very close to Ralph until he passed away.

Paul told me one day how much Ralph reminded him of our father. He used these exact words: "Monie, mi papa favors Ralph because Ralph has always been loving and respectful to Father. He has never heard him say any offensive statements to our father in public or private. Ralph has always been there for Father. He was there for him when father went to the hospital with a broken hip. If father needed anything, Ralph was there for him. When father went to the hospital, Ralph would go every day to see him and keep him company. Ralph was there when dad died. Ralph truly loved our father with all his heart. Ralph felt loneliness after his death. He felt like the world had come to an end. He loved to tell Father how the people loved his music and Father was very proud of him for his accomplishments as a musician. They could talk for an hour on music." This I can say, that Ralph also remained a faithful brother to Paul. When Paul passed away, Ralph was also there with him until his last breath. Ralph used to go visit Paul three or four times a week when he was ill. Paul, our brother, died of leukemia. I will give my personal account of my brother Ralph as I grew from a teenager to manhood.

First, I will start in saying that I have been close to my brother Ralph as a teenager. Ralph used to work at the cotton gin in Scottsdale, Arizona. As a matter of fact, Juan Demarbiex, who was married to my sister Betty, worked there also and they used to drive together every day from Tempe to Scottsdale in Ralph's automobile. What I write is the truth, not trying to do any harm to his family or to create any malice against any of them. As I can remember about Ralph when he was in his twenties is this. Every Saturday I used to get his water ready by heating it in a big tub. He would take a hot shower when he got home from work at noon on Saturdays. He would pay me a quarter to get his water ready. One day he asked me if I could take the little rock pebbles out of his hair, he would give me a penny for each one I took out. Sometimes, I would take out more than fifty pebbles. I was making more money in removing the pebbles than getting his water ready. I found out that this helped him relax and he would fall asleep for an hour then he wake up and ask, "Monchie, how many did you take out?" I would be honest with him even though he slept through the whole thing. I took so many and show him the little pebbles and he would pay me without hesitation.

This I did until he got married to Connie Huerta. This little money provided me with movie and candy money every Saturday. I was ten years of age at that time. I also shined shoes in the street downtown Tempe. When he got married, I missed that chore I did for him every Saturday. After he got married, he moved to Los Angeles, California, to work at General Dynamics, Convair Division. Lolita was already living in Los Angeles with her husband Paul Varela. Connie and Ralph moved with them into their apartment. Paul also worked at the same plant with Ralph. Ralph got the job because Paul was a good worker and he spoke for our brother Ralph being a good worker. Ralph was always a very hard worker always. Our father taught all of his children never to lie down on the job. Always give your boss more than one hundred percent per day and also to tell him thanks for giving me a job. We have carried that tradition in the Chavarria family even today. None of our family children have every taken it easy on their jobs. They all have received awards for their work.

Ralph received his army induction papers to report for services to our country. This was in 1942, six months after the Japanese bombed Pearl Harbor. His wife, Connie, came back to Phoenix, Arizona, to live with her parents and to have her first baby. This is my nephew Ernesto (Ernie). Ralph was transferred to the army air force and they trained him as a firefighter. He was assigned to the Manhattan Project. This is the Army Air Force 8th/9th Air Force Squadron that dropped the first atomic bomb in Hiroshima, Japan. He told me that the B-29 that dropped the atomic bomb took off from the air base at Titian Islands. He told me, "Monchie, there were three B-29s that took off that morning. Nobody knew which one had the bomb. But I knew what plane had the bomb. It was the third one that had the bomb. That B-29 took the entire runway and almost went over the edge of the water because it was heavier than the other two that had taken off before." Ralph was telling me the truth on this. After many years after the war, they wrote a book about the dropping of the atomic bomb. The book describes the events that led to the manufacturing of the bomb, where the bomb was assembled, and what B-29 was the one carrying the atomic bomb. It read that the last plane had it on board and they were sweating the mission. For a moment, they though that the plane was not going to make it into the air. Ralph was at the end of the runway with the rest of the other firefighters in case something happened. It was written, that if the B-29 carrying the bomb would have failed to take off of the runway, the whole Island of Tinian would have been blown to bits without survivors. The whole island would have been blown off the map. After the war was over, Ralph came home safe and found employment with the City of Phoenix as a maintenance repairman on a City of Phoenix housing project named Marcus De Niza. He stayed with the City until he retired. Ralph and Connie have four wonderful children. They are all grown-up now, married, and have children of their own. They have gone through divorces and gotten remarried. (Most of the Chavarria's have gone through this cycle.) The young people nowadays don't take their marriages seriously like the older generation's "Until death do you part." Maybe it's because they don't marry for love, only for companionship.

All the boys turned to be musicians. They play the piano; two have stayed with the music and one is an auto mechanic. Ernesto (Ernie), the first-born, has played on tours throughout the United States and overseas. He has a music studio in Mesa, Arizona, now. Ernie played with his father's band for years. He started his music career at the age of fourteen playing with his father's band at the Calderon Ballroom on Sixteenth Street and Buckeye Road. The members of this band were Phoenix's best musicians around the late forties until 1990. These band members were Mike Velasquez, lead trumpet; Chalio Dominquez, saxophone; Scottie, trumpet; Ernie Chavarria, piano; Ralph Chavarria, bass fiddle; Hank Arroyo, drums; Louis Estrada, vocalist. Ralph's band played backup music to the most famous singers from Mexico when they came to the United States to perform in Phoenix, Arizona, like Pedro Vargas, Tongolele, Mexico's most famous dancer; she danced to the music of Chapito Chavarria. The band took the name of Chapito Chavarria because Ralph is short, about five feet four inches in height. The people began to call the band Chapito Chavarria and that is how the band became known, "the Chapito Chavarria Band." Though they have all retired now, they are still known as members of that band.

Some have passed away and others are still alive, getting together now and then to play for the fun of it. Ralph's second son, Ralph Jr. (Ralphie), became one of Arizona's most famous piano player, both in classical or modern music. He is also a music composer like his father. Ralphie also played with his father's band. Ralphie has played some of his music that he has composed to me personally. I can honestly say that he is good, real good. One night that he was playing a concert in Phoenix, he was brutally beaten up in the parking lot after the concert by two white karate instructors who didn't like him because of his race and the whites liking his music. The law did find them and they went on trial, but were found innocent of the beating and were freed. Ralphie was diagnosed with a brain damage, never again to play music, besides broken bones. He was in the hospital for three months until he was able to be taken home. Ralphie had to learn how to speak again, because they damaged his vocal cords with karate chops to his throat. He lost his memory also. Ralph and Connie would not give up on their son healing again. They prayed together as a family and individually. Each and every one did their best to show him how much they all loved him by being on his side day and night. After he healed from his injuries, the family started to help him talk, even though the doctors told the family that Ralphie would not be able to talk again because of his injuries to his vocal cords. And most of all, that he would never play the piano again. Through the faith of the entire family in our Father in Heaven and our Lord Jesus Christ, Ralphie started to recover from his injuries. He first started to talk in slurry words, then he began to say the word more clearly. It took a year for him to finally talk clearly and his memories to start to come back. He started telling his mother of what he remembered as a little boy playing with his brother, Ernie, and Barbara, his sister. Then one day, he began to remember what happened to him. The family felt so happy that his memory had come back. One thing was happening to him each day. He started to have very severe headaches and the doctor gave him some medication that made it worse. One clear day, he went to town (downtown Phoenix) with his mother. While he was waiting for her outside of the store, he saw and heard this young man talking to a group of people. He walked over to see what was he talking about, and he heard him talking about the word of God and his son Jesus Christ as our Savior. He told his mother what he had just heard and Connie, his mother, told him that God would heal his children if they believed in his son Jesus Christ.

He said to his mother, "Mom I believe in his word and I would like to do his will." When they got home, Ralphie went into his room and came out with all his medicines, and told his mother, "Mom I don't need these anymore. The Lord has healed me, I don't have the headache anymore." And he threw them into the kitchen sink and flushed them down with water. To this day, that I know of, He has never taken any more pills for his headaches. They have completely gone. Now he has joined with these young groups that belong to the church of this young man that he heard preaching. He has also returned to playing the piano. He is a better piano player than before his injuries. He has composed five songs to God in praising him for his healing powers. When he plays those songs, you can feel the presence of our Father in Heaven within you. He has played those songs for me personally and has asked me if he has done the right thing. Of course he has, he has devoted his life in helping people and telling them of Jesus Christ. He has also gone to playing the piano for famous music groups that come to Phoenix; he does not participate in any evil things. After he is done playing, he goes home and stays away from any activities that are against the word of God.

Chapter 26

Not all of Ralph's sons followed on the Chavarria music legacy. Michael became an auto mechanic. He is considered as one of Phoenix's best Rolls-Royce mechanic.

Michael, the last born, also learned to play the piano like his brothers. He plays only for his enjoyment. He is a comedian playing the piano. He plays all kinds of music but he jokes while he plays, like the great pianist Victor Borges. He doesn't play with his brothers together. Though he's good at the piano, he doesn't take it seriously. He prefers to work on automobiles. Michael turns out to be one of Phoenix's top Rolls-Royce mechanic. People that own Rolls-Royce in the valley come to the garage were he is employed and ask that he work on their automobile nobody else. All of us Chavarrias are very proud of Ralph's sons and his only daughter Barbara. This family of my brother Ralph Sr. is a very close family. They are all married and have children, but the family still sticks together if one of them needs help. All of us give the credit to Connie. She has stuck with the family through thick and thin. She has always been there for all of them. Yes, she has had her share of disagreements with her husband Ralph. But I'll say this about her, Connie, she is one woman that has a mind of her own. She will say what's on her mind, either you like it or not. I feel that if she had been a weak mother, the family would not have lasted, and the closeness they now have wouldn't be there. My brother Ralph has been a good provider for the family and loved his family. I don't intend to take away any credit from Ralph, my older brother, but the credit goes to Connie for keeping the family together. Ralph was always playing music with his band, "all over Arizona." He really didn't spend much time at home with his family as they grew up.

Chapter 27

Ramon writes about Beatriz (Betty), what she went through in her early years of growing up and later concerning her marriage to John Demarbiex, her involvement with Ben Gamboa while married to John Demarbiex, and what happened to her when John found out of her extramarital affair with Ben Gamboa.

What I remember about my big sister Beatrice. We all in the family called her Betty. She was already married to Juan "John" Demarbiex when I was born at the railroad yard. I was one year older than Billy, her firstborn child. As a matter of fact, Billy and I grew up together almost. At this time, it was 1937. I was nine or ten years old when they moved to Scottsdale, Arizona. As a matter of fact, Billy went to kindergarten school with me and Helen, Betty's second child. What I remember about Betty; she was nineteen years older than me. She was a very beautiful girl. Even though she was already a mother at that age, she was always being approached by men for a date. This what I'm going to write is not a secret concerning what happened to Betty before my mother passed away.

My mother, Rita, was very close to Dad's first children by his first wife, Dolores Amado Chavarria. All of you must remember that in the beginning of the Chavarria history, I wrote how my mother met my father and how old the children were. Mother was almost like their mother and she loved them as if they were her own, so she was always concerned with their happiness. I was about eight years old when this happened. I will try to give an accurate account of what I saw and heard. One Sunday morning in the summertime, Mom and I were going to church. We were walking from 520 West First Street to the Catholic church (Mount Carmel) located at the corner of College Avenue and University Street in Tempe, Arizona. The Tempe Railroad Train Station was between our house and the Town of Tempe. Betty, Juan, and the children lived on the other side of the railroad tracks just off the tracks about 200 feet.

I remember walking with mom when she said to me, "Let's stop at Beatrice, and see if the children are going to church. They can go with us and let Juan and Beatrice sleep a little more." My mother was a very devoted Catholic. She never misses mass on Sundays and she always took us children with her to church. Why the rest didn't go that Sunday, I don't remember. All I remember was that we were the only two going to church that Sunday. When we arrived at Betty's house, mother noticed that the front of the yard close to the front door to the house had blood on the ground. She knocked on the front door and called Betty's name. Nobody answered her. Then the landlord came walking to my mother and said to her, "Rita, Beatrice is in the hospital in Mesa. Juan is in jail, and the children are here with us." Then my mother asks Juan Lopez, the landlord. Juan was the owner of two houses at the back of his that he rented. My sister and her husband rented from him. Juan's family was very close friends of our family. One of his sons, Lucio Lopez, became my close buddy until he died this year (2005). Mr. Lopez related to my mother what he and his wife saw happened. They saw Juan, Betty's husband, come home around 7:00 AM that morning. They heard a scuffle outside on the backyard. They came out to see what was happening. This is what he, Mr. Lopez, said to my mother. "Rita, I saw Juan and Ben Gamboa fighting on the backyard, Ben had a knife on his hand. He was trying to cut Juan, Juan managed to get a hold of Ben's arm and take the knife away from him and Juan said to Ben, 'go home I don't want to fight you.' Ben did not take Juan's warning and came at him. Juan had Ben's knife in his right hand and when Ben came after him, Juan swung the knife across Ben's stomach and Ben went down on his knees and his guts hanging out."

"Then we saw Juan go inside the house and started beating Beatrice. They came outside and Beatrice was hitting Juan with her hands. Juan then really got angry, and started hitting Beatrice with his fist and knocks her down and started kicking her all over." This is when the landlord stepped in to stop Juan from kicking Betty to death. After Juan, he called the police and ambulance to come and take Beatrice to the hospital. This is what I heard of what happened there that morning from the landlord. I remember my mother telling Juan Lopez, "Juan, take care of the children until I get back." We head to the Tempe City Hall because the jail was underneath the city hall and there was a window, one could talk to the prisoners there. When we got there, mom called Juan to come to the window and Juan responded, "Rita, I'm very glad that you came." When Juan came to the window, Mother asked him, "What happened, Juan?" This is his side of the story. I know this for a fact. I was there holding my mother's hand as she talked with Juan. "Rita, I got sick at work. (Juan and Ralph, my brother, worked together at the Cotton Gin, in Scottsdale, Arizona.) The boss told me to come home and see if some bed rest would help me to get well." Raphael, as Juan used to call our brother Ralph, told him, "Go home, don't worry about me. I'll find a ride to go home." Ralph used to ride to work with Juan, our brother-in-law.

Then he said to my mother, "Rita, when I opened the door into the house, I found Ben Gamboa in bed with my wife. They both woke up scared. I told Ben to get dressed and leave and I stepped into the kitchen, so both could put some clothes on. I had the door opened so Ben could go out. (The house had only one door to enter, this was through the kitchen.) Ben came out into the kitchen and saw that I was holding the door open for him to leave. But instead of leaving, he pulled a knife out and tried to cut me. I grabbed his arm and we went outside struggling with the knife. I made him drop the knife and we trade punches. I knocked him down and bent over to pick the knife. He got up and told me that he had been having an affair with my wife for the last six months while I was at work. This got me very angry. He wasn't satisfied in telling me this. I told him to go home and we would settle this some other time. He told me that I was afraid of him, he wanted to settle it now and he came at me, having the knife in my hand, I took a switch across his belly and cut him good. Ben went down on his knees holding his stomach with both hands. Rita, his guts came out of his belly as he laid on the ground hollering, believing that he was going to die. I went back into the house to talk to the wife why was she doing this to me. She told me the same thing Ben told me about their affair. She started hollering at me and I started to walk outside. Beatrice came after me with a big kitchen spoon, hitting me on the head and back. That really got me angry hearing her defend Ben. I closed my hands and started to hit her in the face and stomach. She fell down and I started kicking her all over until she couldn't move. That's when I noticed Mr. and Mrs. Lopez holding Ben's stomach with some form of clothing. They asked me, 'What happened Juan?' I didn't answer them. I remember that I said, 'Can I use your phone to call the police and the ambulance?' They gave me permission to use the phone. When I called the police, I told them what had happened and they said if an ambulance was needed. I said yes and they were the ones that got the ambulance. The Lopezes told me that they would take care of the children until one of the families would pick them up. Rita, I don't know what's going to happen to me." I do remember that mother told him that she was going to take care of them, not to worry.

Juan was release two weeks later. He was found to be innocent of what happened. There was no assault charges filed against him by Ben or Betty. They stayed married for a number of years and had another girl born to them, Marie Roberta. John and Betty finally got divorced and both married to different persons. This is hard to believe, but Betty married Ben Gamboa and stayed together two years, and got divorced and both of them married again to different persons. The reason for the divorce of my sister Betty and Juan was that Helen, their daughter, was beaten and raped by four white rich boys and after her healing, had to go to a metal institute for the insane.

While she was being treated at the hospital, she became acquainted with the gardener, who happens to be Ben Gamboa. When Betty used to go visit Helen at the hospital, she also saw Ben and didn't tell Juan, her husband, and when he finally found out that Betty and Ben had conversations at the hospital, he divorced my sister Betty for not telling him that she was seeing Ben again. Betty married again after her divorce to a Pete Castro and stayed with him until he passed away after seven years of marriage. Betty passed away in the year 2000, at the age of ninety-two.

I have always loved my sister Betty. When I grew up and learned how to drive, I used to go visit Billy. We go and buy some beer, Billy knew some guys who were old enough to buy beer and they would buy Billy a six pack. Later, when I came home from the service, I was already married. I would go visit him and we would go where my sister worked as a waitress. She would keep an eye on us because Billy was also married and we would dance there. She made sure that we didn't mess around with any of the girls. She would go to our table and tell us, "It's time for both of you to go to your wives." We would walk to her house and shoot the breeze for a while and I come home. She always made sure that I didn't take anyone home. She knew what can happen if you do. I'm very thankful to her for taking care of me. May she rest in peace. I have also done her Temple endowments as getting her seal to her father and mother. I'm trying to find Juan's records to have her seal to him for time and eternity in the house of the Lord.

Chapter 28

Ramon writes about his brother Alfredo and how Alfredo took over the chores of taking care of his small brothers and sister. Ramon tells what happened to Alfredo and why he left the family and became a hobo.

When I started writing the family history, Alfredo was still alive. He was working at La Costa, California, near San Diego. He was the landscaping contractor at the golf course at the famous La Costa Resort. While he was working there, he had a stroke that he had to go into the hospital for treatment. My brother Alfredo never recovered and passed away a few days after. Before he died, my wife, Margaret, and I went to visit him at the hospital. He was able to talk and we had a long conversation concerning our youth. This is what I recollect of my brother Freddie, as all of us call him. Freddie played a very important part of our lives, which is on the children of my father's second marriage to our mother, Rita Moreno Chavarria. When Rita, our mother, passed away on 10 August 1937, Alfredo quit school in order to take care of all of the family. He became to us like a second mother. There was nothing he didn't know what to do. Everything women could do in caring a family, our brother could do. He was a very good cook. We really enjoyed his cooking plus cleaning the house, and washing and ironing our clothes for school and church. He also sends us to school with lunch. Alfredo didn't like us kids going to an all-white school with dirty clothes. He didn't want anyone making fun of us for being dirty. And because of him, we never had any problems in school or otherwise.

He was always there when one of us children would get sick. He took good care of us on that. If we had to go to the doctor, he takes us there. Of course, father would pay the bills. If one of us children happened to fall down, he would pick us up in his arms and soothe our hurt or treat our wounds with medication. Freddie did this for three years; caring for us and teaching us our school homework. He was always there for us in whatever was needed by us. We were really happy. Freddie made us happy that we didn't miss our mother that bad. He would always tell us, "You got to be good in order to be with your mother someday." I didn't know at that time that my mother had taught Alfredo all the chores of the house. She taught him how to cook different food and how to make tortillas and oven bread.

Alfredo was, like I said before, a great cook. Our lives were really going great; we were a happy family because our brother Freddie made sure that we didn't fight amongst us. I can't remember ever getting spanked by him or see him spank any of the other brothers and my little sister, Josie. This was too good to be believed by us. Our lives came to a halt, changing from good to worse. Out of nowhere, our father, without telling us what he was planning to do, did this for a reason we don't know.

He hired a housekeeper, by the name of Margarita Vidal Montanez. She was a divorcée with six children of her own. This made Alfredo very unhappy because she came in telling him that she was taking over his chores; that he had to go to work and help the family income. Magge, as we called her (Maggie in English), came to our house giving orders like she was the mother of all of us. She was very harsh with us right away. This caught us by surprise, of her coming to work for the family. Alfredo felt betrayed by our father of what he did in hiring Magge to do the housework. He felt that he was too old to go finish school. When he went to our father to tell him why he didn't tell us of his plans to hire a housekeeper, Father got angry and told him that it was not his business of what he was doing this for. He didn't want anybody to ever question him of what to do in his house. We felt the way she started treating us that she didn't like us at all. She would come in to work at ten o'clock in the morning and leave at five. After working for the family for a month as a housekeeper, Father started to take her home at night after she was done for the day. As I can recall, she had been with us for three months when all of a sudden, she started to bring her clothing and staying overnight instead of going home. During all this three months, father started building a small cottage about twenty feet away from the house. After it was finished, he called us to tell us that Rudy and I would be sleeping in the new bedroom he had just finished building; that our little sister, Josephina (Josie), would continue to sleep in the big house. Fito, as we call our brother Rudolpho, and I wondered why we were being tossed out of the big house that was warm during winter months to a cold house without a heater and electricity. After a week, we found out why. Father went on his car to bring Magge to our house one Saturday morning. When they came back to the house, Father got out of the car first, then Magge and a little boy about six years of age, and on the backseat of the car, two girls got out. One was about my age, eleven years, and the other was about fourteen years.

Our father called us to come and greet Magge's children. The little boy was named Gilbert, the girl my age was Dora Louisa, and the fourteen-year-old was named Dalia. Later on, I gave Gilbert the nickname of Coily because he had curly hair, and Dora Louisa the nickname of Licha. We never gave Dalia a nickname. At this time, we thought that they were just coming in for a visit, but then we saw Magge and our father lowering some suit cases from the trunk of the car. That's when our father said, "Magge and the children are moving in with us." I know that we didn't mind that, but we did mind that Magge was going to live at the house. We did mind that, simply because she had already started to mistreat us by hitting us on top of the head and back if we talked back to her or we wouldn't do what chores she gave us to do right away. She also started to lie to our father concerning our conduct with her. She would give us the hardest chores and the girls nothing to do, but she would put our little sister to sweep and wash dishes. When it was time to eat, she would serve more food on the plates of her children than us. To this, we started to complain to her and she got upset and told our father that he had very ungrateful children. Our father took her side on this and told us that next time this would happen, he would take the belt on us. I'll say this in the most honest way there is. For the rest of our growing years at that house, not home, Magge took advantage of her wining our father over with her lie that she would continue too mistreat us in the meanest way she could at the eating table. Alfredo tried to defend us with Father, but our father did not want to listen to him.

Alfredo couldn't take the abuse that Magge was giving us and the way she was also treating him as an outcast. Alfredo got a hold of us, Fito, Josie, and myself, and told us that he was leaving the house and going somewhere else to live. That night, Alfredo left during the night and never came back to the house. When father found out that Alfredo had gone, he called our two brothers, Pablito and Ralph, and told them to go looking for Alfredo and bring him to him. That he would take action against him to where he (Alfredo) would never again embarrass him again. Our brothers went hunting for him for days and never found him. Our brother hopped on a train that night and went back to Solomonville where he was born, found a job washing dishes in a café, and later became the cook there. He found out that his big brothers were looking for him and he again hopped the trains going from place to place as a hobo. Nowadays, one calls this kind of people transients or homeless people. One summer evening, Magge send me to the store for potatoes, beans, and rice. She gave me a five-dollar bill to pay for the groceries. As I was approaching the railroad tracks to cross them, I hear a voice calling me by name. "Monchie, Monchie." I looked into some bushes nearby and I saw my brother Alfredo stood up. I ran to him and we hugged each other. He told me that he hadn't eaten in three days. That's when I said, "Freddie, I got five dollars with me to by some stuff for Magge. Here, take it and go buy some food." Then he said, "What about you? What are you going to tell Magge about not buying the errant that she gave you the money for?" I said, "Don't worry about it. I'll find a good excuse to tell her." I was thirteen at that time. He hugged me and said," Don't tell anyone that you saw me. I'm on my way to Los Angeles to see if I can find Cuca, our sister. Little brother, take good care of your self and I'll see you again someday." Then he took off to a hamburger place that we all bought hamburgers to eat for 15 cents, and that was the last time I saw my brother until he came to Tempe after serving in the Second World War with Germany and Japan. I almost forgot that I saw him just two weeks before the Japanese bombed Pearl Harbor. He came from Los Angeles to see the family before and he gave me my very first Pachuco pants (zoot pants).

Now let me tell you what happened when I got home without the groceries and no five dollars. Magge told me, "What happened? You're all dirty on your face and hands. Where are the groceries?" I remember to this day my answer. "Magge I ran to the store and when I was to pay for the groceries, I didn't find the money in my pocket of my pants, and I went back the way that I ran to the store and tried to find the five-dollar bill; even got on my knees to see if I could see it by the light of the moon. I didn't find it anywhere." Then she calls my father who was playing his violin in the family room. Father came out and Magge told him what had happened. Father asks, "Is this what happened Ramon?" I said, "Yes, Father, I lost the money Magge gave me to bring the groceries she needed." He grabbed me by the arm and took me into the living room. He took his belt from his pants and started hitting me in my butt and back. He said to me, "This will teach you to be more careful next time with any kind of money that is given to you." Yes, it hurt, but I was glad that I had given the money to my brother to eat.

Chapter 29

Ramon tells a little bit of his sister Lolita. She married Paul Varela in the late 1930s. What kind of life they lived in Los Angeles, later in San Francisco, California, the big earthquake in 1949. This was Ramon's first experience of an earthquake.

As far as I can remember, Lolita, whose real name is Dolores, met Paul Varela in Solomonville, Arizona. When we moved to our home on 520 West 1st Street in Tempe, she was already married. I don't recall her living with us at anytime. When she got married, they must have moved to Los Angeles, California. All that I can remember is that after I came home discharged from the air force in 1947, I went to vocational school under the GI Bill in Thunderbird air base in Scottsdale, Arizona. This was in 1947-48 and I enrolled in the courses of Body and Fender Repairman and Auto Painter. After graduating from vocational school, I couldn't find a job in the surrounding areas of Tempe. My wife, Margaret, decided that I go to San Francisco and stay with Lolita until I could send for her. I took the Greyhound bus to San Francisco, California, and when I got there, I called Lolita and she sends Paul to pick me up at the bus station. She sure was glad to see me. We talked for a while and then she said, "Monchie, Fito is here with me," and at the same time she said that Fito (whom we called Rudolpho, his real name, or Rudy) "is staying with us because he separated from his wife, Frances." I ask what happened. "Fito caught her going out with other men while he was at work. He caught her in a hotel room with a sailor. Frances had been doing this for quite a while, Monchie," she said to me. "She would leave the children with her mother. She would lie to her mother that she had to go do some shopping, and go downtown to pick men up." As she was telling me this, Fito came down the stairway and said, "I sort of figured that I recognized your voice, brother."

Fito didn't have to go to work the next day, so we talked till 1:00 AM. Then Lolita told us, "You two should go to bed and get some rest, you can talk tomorrow." We fell asleep right away, when all of a sudden I fell from bed. I said, "Fito, why did you push me out of bed?" He said, "I didn't," when we heard Lolita hollering at us. "Get out of the house, we're having an earthquake!" We ran out of the house to the front sidewalk and we saw the hills moving, houses, streets, and cars up and down. This was my first earthquake in California. After that one, and it was a big one, 6.7 on the Richter scale. It knocked down houses, broke store windows, cars ran down the hill. Lolita and her family lived on top of a hill called Clipper Street and it went down to the main street called Broadway. Boy, what a mess it made. Our sister's house got a few wall cracks, not bad. We all helped Paul, Lolita's husband, to patch them up. Fito took me to try to find a job and I never did find one. So I decided to come to Los Angeles and stay with Alfredo and his family. Fito wanted to come to Tempe, Arizona, to live. He quit his job in San Francisco and they told him, that he was only getting paid for two days, because he didn't give two weeks notice.

He didn't have enough money to get the bus. So I gave him $15 for the Greyhound bus fare to Tempe. He rode with me to Los Angeles and I got down, and he continued to Tempe, Arizona.

Chapter 30

Ramon tells about his stay in Los Angeles, California, how he went through the same trouble about getting a job in Los Angeles, how Alfredo convinced him to stay longer with them and to send for his wife and Baby Rita, what he did in Los Angeles, His feelings of not being able to get a job. Then his trip back to Arizona.

When Fito (Rudolpho) and I arrived at the bus station, Alfredo was already waiting for us. He knew the Fito was going to Tempe, Arizona. He wanted to see him at the bus before he continued on his journey to Arizona. We all three got together outside the bus station and had a nice reunion. This was the last time Alfredo and Fito would see each other alive. We three had a good time talking of the past. Alfredo told us what he did when he left the house and became a hobo. He told us that though he was old enough, he was still afraid the Ralph and Pablito would find him and take him to our father. I told him, "You have already made peace with our father. You went to see him before the war started, don't you remember?"

"Yes, but I didn't see Ralph or Pablo. They might still be upset with me and try to finish what our father wanted them to do." We finally convinced him that it was over. Fito left to Arizona and I went with my brother Alfredo to his apartment. He was renting on a new low-income apartment called Elizo Village on First and Mission.

The apartment was a three bedroom and they were big bedrooms, "not like today." I arrived on a Saturday afternoon and the coming Monday, Alfredo took the day off to help me go looking for a job. We went to the plant he was working, but they were not hiring anyone at that time. He took me all over the area of Los Angeles looking for work that day. No work, so he said, "Let me take you to the employment office and see if they have any employment, and if they don't, you can register for unemployment benefits. They pay good money here for unemployment." Well they sure didn't have any work and they told me, "You are entitled to unemployment because you qualify working in Arizona and never using it." It took three weeks to get my first unemployment check. Alfredo and Ester, his wife, told me, "Monchie, why don't you call Margie and have her come to Los Angeles and you guys can stay here with us until you get a job and then we can help you find an apartment here at the project." I called my wife and send her some money and she and Rita came on the train. The train station was about four blocks away from the housing project. The train station was new and at that time very beautiful.

When I saw my wife and daughter (Rita), at that time we used to call her Bonnie, I was so happy to see them. We went to the housing project and Ester right away took closeness to both of them and told my wife, "My, you're so beautiful; no wonder Monchie didn't let you get away." I can't believe it that all this time (three months) that I could find a job. I started to really get depressed and afraid that I wouldn't be able to support my wife and daughter. I would go looking for miles for any kind of work and couldn't find one at all. Finally, I started to drink with the friends of my brother. I remember one weekend when I went out with Ernie. Ernie was a friend of Alfredo and Ester and was staying with them as a room and board tenant. He was a very nice friend to all of us. When he told me, "Monchie, let's go home." I told him, "You go on. I'm going to walk home and think of what to do since I can't find work." He didn't want me to walk home. But he finally said, "Well, if that's what you want, I let you walk home." I remember very well that I stopped at the bridge that went across the Los Angels River. That's where I broke down to cry. I believe at that time that I wasn't man enough to take care of my wife and daughter.

It came to me that maybe I should jump off the bridge and get it over. I was thinking if I did that my wife could find some other man, man enough to take care of them. Then out of nowhere I heard someone say to me, "Go back home and everything will be all right." Then it seemed that I could see myself working at the juice plant where I was working when I went to California. I got home somewhere in the morning . . . My wife, Margaret, thought that I had been drinking all this time. I have never to this day told her that I had thought of committing suicide in Los Angeles. It seems that everything came into place. Roberto, my brother, was going to lose his car of not paying it. He told me that I could have it if I made the payments on it. I told him that I could, and he turned it over to me. That really came handy. My sister Fina (Josie) was also staying with Alfredo for a few weeks and she made the trip with us to Tempe, Arizona. When we got at my wife's parents home, they were very glad to see us back. I went to the plant where I was working before, next day and I asked Mr. Ed Harrington if he had any work for me. He answered, "Ramon, when can you start?" I answered, "Today, if you need me." He said, "You will work on nights until I can put you on days."

Chapter 31

In this chapter, Ramon finds a job in Tempe right away in the same place he worked before going to California. Ramon goes back to San Diego, California, and again loses his job and heads back to Arizona. He finds a job right away at the plant he used to work before going to California.

Since then, I have always been thankful to my Heavenly Father and our Lord Jesus Christ for all my blessings that I have received from his hand. I worked for Mr. Harrington till 1952. Then I went to work for the government at Litchfield Park at the navy's biggest aircraft preservation base in the United States. Until 1955, we came back to California to San Diego. We stayed with Charlie, my wife's brother, and his wife, Adelina (PeeWee). Prior to this, I was to go to Muffett air base in San Jose, California. They were getting ready to close the base. We decided to move to California, because of the opportunities for the children to get a good education, better than Arizona. I left alone to California, after overhauling the motor on my 41 Chevrolet. I left at night so that the motor wouldn't heat up on me on the road. I traveled at the speed of thirty-five miles an hour until I got to San Diego. I was supposed to have just stopped to rest and visit Charlie and his family, then leave to San Jose. Charlie convinced me that there was a lot of work in San Diego. He told me, "I'll take a day off Monday and take you job hunting." He did and at the same time, I applied for unemployment benefits in San Diego. Going home, we stopped at the United States Destroyer Base on 32nd Street, Harbor Drive and I went in to the employment Office (IRD) and got a job in the Paint Department. After two weeks, I came over to Tempe, Arizona for the family. The wife didn't understand how people could live on top of hills and the houses not falling down. She was used to living in flat land, not hilly. She got used to it after awhile. She fell in love with San Diego, and still loves it, though we live in Las Vegas, she still wants to go back to Arizona. We stayed in San Diego until 1958. The Destroyer Base had a big reduction in force and I was caught in it. I could have stayed as a taxi driver, but my eyesight wasn't that good to drive a taxi. I wore eyeglasses but my eyes would get tired. So I had to turn it down and look for a job in San Diego. After looking for employment all around the San Diego area, I couldn't find any; there were people without work because all the aircraft plants had also reductions of workers in 1958. It was a very tough time for all the people in San Diego. I decided to go back again to Tempe, Arizona. We stayed with my wife's parents again and we found a house for rent next to them. I went to work at a body and paint shop in Phoenix, Arizona, and we bought a brand new automobile. Then we saw in the newspaper this finance company that sold houses and would take any automobile as a down payment paid for or not. I gave the car down as a down payment on this nice three-bedroom house in Phoenix. Then I receive a call from the Navy Repair Facility, Litchfield Park, to go to work for them. I told the owner of the body and fender paint shop that I was quitting. Carl Nielson is his name and he is a member of the Church of Jesus Christ of Latter-day Saints. He called me into his office and said, "Ray, you're a good auto painter and I can sure use you after work here and on Saturdays all day. I need you to work for me part-time." I remember that I told him, "Carl, I'll work for you part-time because you have treated me very well here and I would be very honored to continue working for you for all you have done for me." I stayed with the government at Litchfield and Carl until I came back to San Diego In 1961.

We never went back to Arizona again. We found a house for rent right away and later, we found one closer to town and the children grew up in Chula Vista, California. We started active in church in Chula Vista first ward, the children went to primary on Saturdays, and Rita went to seminary from Monday to Friday at 6:00 AM to 8:00 AM. On Tuesday nights, Rita, Raymond, and Jackie went to Mutual (Young Men and Women Youth Program of the Church.). I held different callings in the church. Then I was called to be a Stake Missionary for two years. The Church found us worthy to be sealed to each other in 1962. My wife and I were married for time and all eternity in the Los Angeles Temple and the children sealed to us for all time and eternity. During this time, the children had grown to manhood and womanhood. We encountered problems with a new bishop (Bishop Rison). We had an encounter that almost went to fistfighting inside of the Stake center while general conference was going on. He was giving the family too much work. The church had a contract with a mailing company to stuff envelopes and lick them close for mailing and since we were on church welfare, he had the family stuffing envelopes even on Sunday that the family didn't go to church in order to get six boxes out by Monday. This went on for a month until I found out that other members were getting one box to do instead of six boxes like my family.

I went to see the bishop on this. He got upset with me and told me that members that are on welfare have to earn their keep. I told him, "From this day on my family is through with stuffing envelopes. They will no longer stay away from church and you will no longer have us on church welfare.

The money that I'm donating on fast offerings and tithing will keep my family from starving." Due to other things that happened to us in church, we stopped going to church for many years. I started drinking again, feeling hurt and getting mad at our bishop. Then this bishop is killed on a motorcycle and a new one is called to be the bishop. He was very nice and made all the efforts to bring us back. The children had all grown up and had minds of their own. I have never to this day force them in any way to go back to church. I feel that someday they will return like I have. They have a God-given free agency to choose good or bad. I leave them alone because I understand what they went through. It's hard to be treated the way we were, by those over us in church. I know that the church is true and perfect, but not all the members have a true testimony of its restoration here on the earth in this the latter days. I am in no way claiming that my children are perfect. Rita, Jackie, and Marcia Ann have had their share of problems on this earth. They have all married outside the church and their marriages have not lasted long. They have bore children of these men, but the men they married didn't really love them. To me, these men were only looking at them because of their beauty. They are very beautiful even today. They have maintained their bodies trim and their faces are very young for their ages. I love each one very much and I am very proud of what they have accomplished. Each one has done their thing and very good at what they have worked at. I have never passed judgment on them. I'm their father and always will be. They are mine and the wife; they have been sealed to us for eternities to come.

Now I will write a little about my sons. These three sons are the ones that will carry my legacy of the Chavarria's. Everyone knows that the genes run through the man; daughters marry and the name become secondary. The wife and I are very proud of them. I will write something on each one, their history to me is a proud one. Why? One may ask. They have done much better than I in sports in school. Raymond is the oldest of my sons, so I will give a father's account of his accomplishments. Raymond was born a very good child. I remember in the house that we were renting close to their grandparents, Maria and Gonzalo Perea. He used to meet me at noontime when I go to eat at the house. He would stand on the door until I parked the car and then, he would run out to meet me and I would pick him up and put him on the backseat of the car and give him a ride back and forth. Then he would pick his milk bottle and go play. This was every day that I gave him a small ride. One day when I backed the car with him on the backseat (The car was a Ford convertible.), as I started forward, Raymond went rolling off the car and hit the ground. This gave me such a scare that to this day I really don't know what happened that he went rolling off the backseat. I was driving very slowly as always.

Second big scare I got was on the house we were renting, the electrical wires were installed on the outside of the walls because the houses were built of adobe. It was a one-bedroom, the girls sleep on the bedroom and Mom, Raymond, and I sleep on the front room. One night, Raymond was playing in bed and he fell backward on the bed and tried to grab the electrical wire. He did grab it and pull the wire from the connection and stuck on his little hand. The electricity was burning his flesh on his hand and I grabbed the electrical wire and yanked it from his hand. He was being electrocuted. His little hand smells like burnt meat. He never cried of the pain, we are the ones that cried. He went to high school at Chula Vista Castle Park. He played basketball and he was good at it. Twice he came from behind and shot the winning baskets. The crowd went wild; Raymond was a hero to them. His uncle Chuy was there one time that he won the game in the last three seconds to play. Chuy jumped out of his place and ran to hug Raymond. It was a site to behold. I was so proud of him. All I had to do is give him a smile or Mom and he knew that we were proud and happy for him. He broke many basketball records at Castle Park that still stand on the books to this day. After he graduated from high school, he went to work for the Bell Telephone Company as a linesman. He was drafted to serve in the military during the Vietnam conflict, but was send to Germany instead. He finished his tour of duty and came home, and went to work at the Bell Telephone Company again. Raymond later married Teresa Murielle. She had been married before and when she married Raymond, she was already with a child. This child was her first husband's child. How my son married her pregnant already, I'll never know. I often wonder if he did it to show his former girl Irene that he could find any girl to marry. Teresa had two boys of their own, Anthony Ray and Michael, Teresa's first child was named Bobby. We learned to love all three as grandchildren. What happened to the family is that all of a sudden, Teresa started to change, that led for them to get a divorce. Though my son has never really said what caused the divorce, my conclusion comes that since Teresa was working at this bank, she must have started fooling around with her boss. After the divorce, she married her boss. They never had any children of this marriage. Teresa gave Raymond a very bad time with her divorce. She kept the children from coming over to see us, their grandparents. She would only send Bobby to see us. In truth, we saw Bobby grow to manhood, but not Anthony or Michael. To this day, we have only seen Bobby and Anthony, not Michael at all.

After a year or so, Raymond married Debbie Calabrese. They had a child out of their marriage. My grandson's name is Jason. We went with the same trouble with Debbie's parents. They took our grandson to live with them after Debbie tried to hit my son Raymond on the head with a golf club. Jason saw his mother come from behind Raymond while he and

Jason were watching a baseball game. When Debbie walked in the house and started arguing with Raymond in front of Jason, Raymond didn't pay any attention to Debbie because she was all duped up smoking marijuana with her friends. Our grandson saw her pick the golf club and come from behind Raymond sitting on the sofa. As she raised the club to come down on our sons head, Jason calls at his father to look out. I don't remember if our grandson pushed his father out of the way. Raymond was taken to jail when Debbie called the police. She claimed that Raymond hit her on the face. What really happened was that Raymond was taking his clothes out of the closet to leave and Debbie came at him again taking his clothes that were still hanging on the clothes hangers and she pulled the clothes out of Raymond's hands and some of the hangers scratched her face and she was able to convince the police officers that my son had hit her in the face.

Raymond had to spend the night in jail and I had to go bail him out the next day. The police found out what really happened and no charges were pressed on my son Raymond. That is the only time he has been in trouble. We knew that our son wasn't a woman beater. He was always a kind person and never looked for trouble, but never ran away from it if they look to settle it man to man. Afterward, he got together with Eleanor, didn't last very long and Raymond moved out and at last he found what he had been looking for all this years. He met Jennifer, a divorcee with three small children that works with the same telephone company of Pacific Bell that Raymond worked for and retired. She is a very loveable person and very charming. I went with the wife and I first met her. We immediately fell in love with her. She was the one that we wanted for our son to spend the rest of his life with. Jen, as I call her, has become my daughter, not my daughter-in-law. I don't believe in daughters-in-law or sons-in-law. They become family when they marry into my family. Jen has three beautiful children, two boys and one girl. They all have blond hair and love our son as a father.

Raymond, my son, is a hero to me. He has saved two lives. One was when he pulled a girl from a burning car and never stayed to get any credit. He stayed with the girl until the police and ambulance came to help the girl. Next one was that he and his girlfriend were eating in this restaurant and a customer was eating chicken and a bone stuck in her throat. Nobody knew what to do. The daughter of the lady that had the bone stuck ran to Raymond's table and asked him if he could help her mother. My son went to the lady's table and she was having trouble breathing. She was turning blue, of what he told me. Raymond applied the Heimlich hold. The first try didn't do any good, then he applied more pressure on the second try and out came the bone and the lady was all right. She thanked him for saving her life and she reported this to the Bell Telephone Company and Raymond received a hero's reception with all the employees and the daughter and lady being present and they took their picture with him. Today as a grown man, he is still that little boy as I see him. He is very loveable, respectful, helpful, charitable. Mom and I love him very much, I'm very proud of him, he has accomplished more than I have and that is why I'm so proud of all my boys.

Raymond, my son, I, your father, leave you this blessing. That someday you will return to the church again and take your wife and family and be sealed to them for all time and eternities. That you may dwell in the presence of our Father and Mother and Jesus Christ, our Savior in heaven and with us, your parents, also and the entire Chavarria and Perea families forever. I leave you these blessings in the name of Jesus Christ by the authority of the Holy Priesthood of Melchizedek that I hold in the Church of Jesus Christ of Latter-day Saints, Amen.

Rita Moreno Chavarria

Margarita Perea Chavarria/
Ray Moreno Chavarria

Ray Morena Chavarria age 76/
Margarita Perea Chavarria age 76

Jackie Perea Chavarria

Jackie Perea Chavarria

Marcia Ann Perea Chavarria

Rita Perea Chavarria

Left to right, Margarita Perea Chavarria, Charlie Perea, Maria Perea Bariga, Jesus Perea

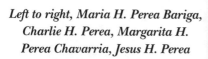

Left to right, Maria H. Perea Bariga, Charlie H. Perea, Margarita H. Perea Chavarria, Jesus H. Perea

Airman First Class, Ray Moreno Chavarria

Left to right, Davy William P. Chavarria (second son), Michael P. Chavarria (third son), Raymond P. Chavarria (first son)

Jackie Chavarria and her dad Ray Chavarria

left to right Michael Chavarria, Evelia Delayo, Davy William Chavarria

Abelardo Alvarez, My father Pablo Chavarria, Juan Dembarbiex

Private 1st class, Ray Chavarria

left to right Ray Chavarria, Adolpho Alvarez, Jesus Perea. Edward Flores, back row Rudy Flores

*Left to right Lucio Lopez,
Ray Chavarria, Don Moraga*

*My brother
Antonio (Tony) Chavarria*

Chapter 32

Ramon talks about his son Davy. He tells of things he saw his son do and accomplish as a young boy and later in manhood and why Davy should always be proud of his contribution to the family. Mom and Dad always think of Davy as a Good Samaritan.

Now I write about my second son, Davy William. Raymond gave him the name of Davy, mom and I added the name William. Raymond loved to see Davy Crocket, King of the Wild frontier on TV. My son Davy has made the entire family proud of him. Not only was he a good son as he was growing up. Davy as a little boy started to show his talents. He was and still is very knowledgeable of many things in this world today. As a little boy, he started to draw pictures out of funny books. He did not trace them, he draw them with his own mind. I still have in my possession some of his drawings he draw for me on Father's Day when he was a little boy. The pictures are Snoopy, Charlie Brown, Linus, and Lucy, since he was a little boy, he has printed like a typing machine. He prints very beautifully. He was very helpful around the house as a small boy. He helped me clean the yard, and as he grew up, he would mow the lawn for me. Davy was very quiet as a boy. He likes to study quite a bit. When he started school, he became very smart bringing A on all his schoolwork. Mom and I didn't have to tell him to do his schoolwork. He comes home from school, have a little snack, and then he would do his schoolwork assignment. Then he goes to play outside with the rest of the children. My son Davy was a good sportsman, as a matter of fact, all three boys were very good at sports. Davy was very good at basketball in school and church. He was always trying to help the team win. One of the actions I saw was when he was on his senior year in high school (Chula Vista High), Davy was really on target that night. He was making all his baskets that he shot. He was really hot that night. Then I saw Davy come off the basketball court to the bench.

He was taken out by the coach, and he put in Davy's place a young Caucasian, who wasn't half as good as Davy. The spectators looked in confusion wondering why they had taken my son out. Then I saw Davy stand up and walked off the gym. Fifteen minutes later, he came over to the stands and sit with me. I ask, "What happened? Why aren't you playing with the team?" He said, "I'm not playing basketball with them anymore. The guy they put in my place, his father donated so much money to the school and told them he wanted his son to play that night." The school lost that game when they were ahead with twelve points when they took Davy out. My son was a man of his word; he never played again for the remainder of the scheduled games they had left. I wanted to go and talk with the coach, of why take my son out and put a player whose father had just donated money to the school. Davy said to me, "Dad, don't worry. Let them have it their way. They aren't going to the finals." He was right, without him, they lost the six games they had left.

When Davy graduated from school, he went to work with Golden Construction in San Diego. Golden Construction is a big company that builds tall buildings and all kinds of houses and freeways. My son started on the yard and worked his way to the outside team of correcting imperfections on homes. They saw that he had knowledge of blueprints and they would send him out to check some of the layouts of homes to make sure of the specified specifications and landscaping code. My son Davy wanted to work for the United States government like me. So I helped him fill an application for employment at the U.S. Naval Air Station at North Island where I worked. With his work experience he had acquired at Golden Construction, he got hired. He started as a sheet metal worker, was picked up to attend the apprentice program. Graduated as an aircraft evaluator on repair, was promoted to procurement officer. He is now four years of retirement. He has been given numerous awards for his work. Mom and I are very proud of him. Davy married his high school sweetheart Diana Beatty and they have both accomplished quite a lot. They both worked hard on their jobs. They have two homes and five acres of prime land in Apple Valley, California. One of the homes he bought for us here in Las Vegas, Nevada is about fifteen minutes from the Las Vegas Strip.

Davy and Dee, as we all call her, come to visit us quite often here in Las Vegas. I am very proud of their accomplishments and so are their brothers and sisters. My son Davy and Dee have been like second parents to my children. Anytime that they needed help, both of them have helped them out. I pray that someday Davy will return to church and take Dee with him and get sealed to each other for time and all eternity in the temple of the Lord. I leave my blessings that if he does go to the temple of the Lord, he and Dee will have many children of their own in the world to come. I leave this blessing in the name of Jesus Christ and by the power of the Holy Melchizedek priesthood Amen.

Chapter 33

Ramon remembers Michael, his last-born son. Michael was always remembering the instructions of his parents. He had a mind of his own, always wanting to hear the truth of questions in life. He was also a sports player in school and church and was always a worker helping his father around the house like his big brothers. He tells how his determination got him to fulfill his dream of becoming a fire captain.

Michael, my last-born son, is a person with a good heart like his two brothers. Since a little boy, he always followed his brothers and sisters around the house observing everything they did. He started to learn real fast what to do around the house. Yes, one might say that the brothers and sisters had him spoiled. They still love him like when he was a little boy. To all of them, they see him as their little baby brother even though he's about six feet three inches tall.

My son Michael has always been the strongest of all the boys. When he was a little boy, he showed that he could take care of himself against other children, he wasn't afraid to defend himself against anyone that would pick on him. He is still that way today. Maybe he took after me in defending himself against those that believe in hurting others. He is also like his brothers and sisters. He does anything that is good to help that person.

When he went to school, he used to take toys to share with the children in school. His mother spoiled him. She used to take him to Tijuana, Mexico, just to eat breakfast, since we lived close to the Mexican border. We lived in San Ysidro, California. We moved from Tempe, Arizona to California when Michael was born in Arizona. As a matter of fact, all my children were born in Arizona except one; Marcia Ann (Dody) is the only one that was born in California. Mom, as I call my wife, used to take him everywhere as a little boy with her, Michael used to ride in the front seat with her and he would stand, not sit, put his little hands behind the front seat, and hold himself and brace himself against turns and stops his mother made. He reminded me of George Washington crossing the Delaware River during the Revolutionary War. Michael was also good at basketball. He was as good as his brothers on the court. All three sons played excellent basketball at school and church.

After graduation, Michael went to vocational training at Jobs for Progress, a nonprofit agency under the American GI Forum. They train you on the job and after, they place you on the same type of training you had been trained to do. Michael was placed at Sanyo, a Japanese company. From there, he went to the Naval Air Station, North Island, San Diego, California. My son was trained as a heavy machine operator. Then at North Island, he was chosen to the apprentice program as a sheet metal mechanic. Being a nonveteran, he was laid off and went to work at Convair as a machine operator. My son was a good worker at Convair. He was hired because he knew how to operate the big machine in the metal shop. They couldn't find a person to operate the machine. After I retired from the Naval Air Station, North Island, I went to work at Convair when Michael was employed there and I used to go visit him at his shop. Michael was called back to North Island as a firefighter after going through firefighting school in college. I have had the pleasure to have worked with two of my sons, Davy William and Michael. Both are still working at the Naval Air Station at North Island at this time as I write my history here in Las Vegas, Nevada, where we moved from San Diego, California, after fifty years living there. My son Michael is a fire captain now. I'm very proud of his outstanding record as a federal employee and as a man. He is a proud father of two sons and a daughter (Kevin, Kyle, and Eva Sofia). I can never write enough of my love for my three sons and three daughters. They have all given me all their love and respect as a father, including their mother. It took me quite a while to find the girl that I would fall in love with and be the mother of my children. The day that I saw her (Margarita Perea), I fell in love with her than at that moment and to this day October 18, 2005. I love her more than when I saw her holding a stop sign in her school safety patrol assignment.

Chapter 34

In this part of my history, I will reveal to my family what were my dreams of helping people get their lives more successful and how I plan to help them with my education. I had good relationships with politicians during my life.

I have always dreamed of having a job helping people find better employment, then working in the cotton fields around the valleys. I often wondered as a teenager why go to school if one is going to work on the farms. If you work on the fields, you don't need an education to pick cotton or work the lettuce fields. I did accomplish my dream of helping people. I wasn't alone on this. I give much of my credits to my wife, who was behind me a hundred percent. She would counsel with me when I had a tough problem with a manager at work or in the community with work programs managers. But most of all was the inspiration of Almighty God. Every morning that I reported for work, I would close my office door from the inside and have a word of prayer, asking Him for help and inspiration to do the job to the best of my abilities and keep his commandments. I thank my Father and our Lord Jesus Christ, for helping me become so successful on the position that I held with the government.

In the position that I held as affirmative action officer at North Island, I had the privilege of going to different states and meeting very important people in our federal government, State and City government. I still communicate with these persons. Some are still in those positions they held when I did business with them in finding employment or training for their people in the San Diego community. I developed a training concept after my retirement from the government to train people who are on welfare and unemployment nationwide. At the time of this writing, March 7, 1997, Vice President Al Gore has it in his hands. I haven't received it back or any input on it. I had this concept working here in San Diego and it saved the government over twenty million dollars on training funds. Later I did get funded to put it to work in San Diego. But the Hispanic community thought that I was trying to put them out of business and they tried to steal the money and Congressman Duncan Hunter returned the Department of Labor check back to them and I was left with no funds. This is the way, some of my so-called friends paid me, and after helping, they become successful in their training programs. "Pure jealousy in their hearts because of my knowledge in training concepts." I have met in private with two presidents of the United States of America. President Richard Nixon and President Ronald Reagan. These meetings were to provide them with information concerning the illegal aliens coming into the United States from Mexico and the problems of the American Indians. I have made friends with Congressmen Duncan Hunter, Randy "Duke" Cunningham, Brian Bilbray, all Republicans from San Diego, California, as well as Senator John McCain from Arizona, Senator Phil Gram from Texas, and the Honorable Speaker of the House of Representatives, Newt Gingrich, also Republicans. I am also a registered Republican and have been asked by the Republican National Committee twice to run for the office of congressman. Twice I had to decline due to lack of funds for a strong campaign to win. One has to put his own money in the primary elections ($70,000). It is very hard for a blue-collar worker to have that kind of money. Though I was unable to run, I helped the two persons who ran, and did get one position as congressman. I felt honored that at least they had called me to run for congressman. The reason for my success is my wife, Margarita. She has always believed in me and has had the faith in me to be successful in my projects. She has endured many hardships in the course of our marriage. I feel very blessed to have her as my wife; they don't come any better than her. She is a smart woman and mother and has taken a backseat to my recognition in public and my accomplishments in life. I honestly believe she was put in this earth to be my wife and to be my helpmate. She has a tremendous faith in God and Jesus Christ. As one can see, I have had many friends in life who have also helped me to be the kind of person who is there if you need a friend to help. I also thank them for the success that I have had in life.

As for my children, they have been the best. I am very proud of their accomplishments at work and at their play. I don't have the least doubt that I have the very best sons and daughters on this earth. And now their children are making us all proud. My grandchildren and great-grandchildren are making me and the wife the most proud because of what they are turning to be in their life. Yes, I have been blessed many times. I feel that the love of our children is the most precious gift a human being can give another. My grandchildren are now giving us that love also. I pray always that our Father in Heaven and our Lord Jesus Christ will always protect them and pour their spirit on each one. My wife and I feel that because of this love from our children and grandchildren, the Lord has blessed us with more days on this earth. I truly believe in his word. He says, "Honor thy mother and father that their days may be prolonged on this earth." My family is obedient to this commandment. When my father was in the hospital in

1973, just before his death in the same year, he told me some of his history. He started to tell me part of his own life when he was a young man. How he loved music and learned to play the violin, but his heart was also in farming. He said, "Son, any time you can do some farming. You will appreciate life more. The love you put into the earth when you plant something. The earth will return it to you with a beautiful result that you will feel full of joy."

Life is that way; what you put into your life that is what you get back. Never expect something for nothing. Always go out of your way and do the best you know how. Someday when you least expect something, a favor is returned or a hand is given to you as you need help. As an adult, I have found this to be true. My whole family will see this truth later as I needed help from different offices of our government and State offices. Our father told me he bought the small ranch he had in rural Tempe, Arizona, because the place reminded him of his father's land in Solomonville, Arizona, where he was born in 1882 on his father's ranch. Father mentioned to me that his father (grandfather) and his two brothers, namely Trinidad and the youngest named Regino, had 2,400 acres of land. The land belonged in the beginning to our great-grandfather Francisco, Indian chief of the White Mountain Coyoteros (Apaches). This land was situated east of Safford, Arizona, all the way to San Jose, Arizona, on both sides of the Gila River. As I continue on the family history, I will be revealing to the whole family how our great-grandfather received this land and what happened that the family is not in possession of it now. For now, I want to finish a part of my history when I was in junior high school.

Chapter 35

In this chapter, the family will know the truth why I started to drink and fight at an early age. Our father was not easy to get along with. He wasn't that way until my mother died.

The three years that I attended junior high school, I was an A student in all my subjects. I passed my test on the Arizona Constitution and the United States Constitution with an *A*. I was chosen to give the class address speech on graduation night. One week before we graduated, we were playing soccer ball at noon and this white boy by the name of Frank Skelton kicked this Mexican guy, smaller than him on the leg chin, instead of the ball. I saw it and got mad of what he had done to Don Cortez. When he had the ball (Frank), I went after him and done the same thing he did to Don Cortez. He laid on the grass hollering until one of the teachers assigned to watch over the playground came over to see what had happened. I told the teacher what Frank had done to Don deliberately. The teacher didn't say anything to me, but he went and told my class teacher Pop Holdeman. He called me outside of the classroom into the area outside the school. He asked what happened out there on the playground as I began to explain to him what happened. My friend Lucio came out to join us and try to help explain what he saw Frank do to Don Cortez. Before I had a chance to face Pop Holdeman, he just raised his hand and slapped me across my right cheek.

I got so mad at him that I went after him to beat him up like he had done to me. But thanks to Lucio, he got hold of me and won't let me go after him. That act caused me not to be the speaker on graduation night. At this time, I was already drinking hard liquor. My father had already been with Magge for four years and I was being treated unkindly by her. My drinking developed due to the problems at home, not at school. In school, I was the top athletic player in all sports: softball, basketball, football, soccer ball, and track. I was well-liked by all the students at the school. My favorite game was football. I played running back because I loved running with the ball and I was good at it. I was so good that the football coach of the high school came over to see me and the school principal to see if I wanted to practice with the high school team for the following year. I

believed that I was going to go on to high school at that time. So I said yes
to Coach Henshew. Every day after school, I would walk over to the high
school, dress up in my football uniform, and go out and practice.

Coach Henshew built the team around me. But the day that I was going
to register for school, I met a great disappointment. I got up early in the
morning and dressed up. Father asks, "Where you going all are dressed up?"
I said, "Father, I'm going to go register for school this morning. It's going
to start in one more week." He said to me, "You're not going to school. You
have to go work and help the family. You had enough school anyway to get
along now." I tried to reason with him. It did me no good to talk to him.
That was the end of my hopes and dreams of being somebody in this world.
I also had plans to go to college and become a lawyer someday, a judge. I
really liked law. I wanted to defend people who got into trouble. That day
of registration, everyone was looking for me at school. They wondered what
happened to me that day. When I did go, it was to get a work permit. I really
felt low that day. Everyone that knew me was wondering what happened
to me. I told the coach what had happened and he said, "It's too bad that
your father feels that way. You could have gone and become somebody here
in Tempe." I was so hurt that I really started to drink heavily on weekend.
Father would take all my earned money and give me a dollar. Lucio would
also get some money from his father and we'll find someone in town to buy
us some beer. A six-pack of beer was $1.36. Later we started buying whiskey
and beer. We would find beer bottles and soda pop bottles, sell them, and
get some drinking money.

Lucio, my buddy, was going through the same thing with his father.
My father wasn't drinking the money he got from me, but Lucio's father
was. He buys all his friends that worked with him at the Hayden Flower
Mill drinks every day. I worked around the valley picking cotton, hawing
cotton, lettuce, cantaloupe, watermelon, broccoli, picking oranges and
grapefruit. Then I got a job with Mr. Charley Tedlock out on the field steady
work. Mr. Tedlock had a contract with the Orange Product Company to
dry and grind the grapefruit peeling and make feed for the cattle. I was
saving some money that I kept from my father. Why? You might ask. Father
would take all of my money on payday and give me a measly dollar for me
to spend. The rest of the fathers would do the same with their working
sons or daughters. It was the way they were brought up in Mexico. What I
did to hide some of my hard-earned money was that I got paid in cash and
we worked different hours every day. So my father really didn't know how
much I was earning. So I would hide $5 every chance I would get. That was
the only way that I could save some money of my own.

My father never found out what I was doing, saving some of my own
money. My other friends did the same thing in keeping some of their

money also. I can say this honestly. What all of us were doing never came out. Our parents believed in the old ways. They believed that the children living with them had to help support the rest of those living at home and the father was the keeper of the money since he was the head of the family. They bought the food and clothing for the children until you left home to get married. One did not leave home at the age of eighteen like today. You left home to start your own family if you were man enough to take the responsibilities of a married man. This is what happened to me at home. After saving this money at the age of seventeen, I gave it to my father to keep for me. I will never forget that I gave my father two hundred dollars to save for me. (This money was going to go to my wedding to Margarita. I had already asked for her hand in marriage.) This was about six months before our wedding date. I asked my father for the money and he said, "What money?" I told him, "The one that I gave you to save for me for my wedding." This is what he said to me, "That money is gone. Mage used it for the needs of the house." I said to my father, "That money was not for the needs of the house, it was for my wedding. I intended to make a big wedding fiesta for Margarita." He just said, "I don't have it anymore and that was it." He didn't care one bit about my wedding. This is when I believed that he never cared enough for me to have a nice wedding. I found out later, that Mage was the one that spent it on her own children, not on the needs of the family. It was her family that benefited from my money. Good thing that I also gave Margarita $50 to save for her wedding suit, she used that money for her outfit. It was light blue and a little hat that went with the outfit. She looked very pretty in it. She looked like a doll, a very pretty doll. We got married with $68 in my pocket. Her father and mother were the ones that came up with the money to give us, and our friends something to eat at our wedding.

To our surprise, all of our friends came to the wedding that was held at my wife's home. My own father came over with some of his musicians and played at our wedding. It was, as it turns out, a very nice wedding after all. I was wrong about my father not caring about my wedding. It was Mage behind the whole thing of spending my wedding money. She didn't show up at our wedding. That I didn't care if she did or not, it didn't bother me one bit. To this day, I remember like it was today. Mom deserved a big church wedding with bridesmaids and chaperons and picture taking of our wedding. All this happened because of my father and Mage. This I have never been able to forget. My wife deserved a big wedding with all the trimmings that goes along with a wedding. I suppose that Mage felt that she got even with me for telling my father about her extra activities behind my father's back. Now that I have given an account of my wedding let me give you an account how I met this beautiful woman that became my wife.

Chapter 36

Ramon tells how he met his wife. He tells about the problems he had with her former boyfriend from Mesa, Arizona and how the Mesa Pachuco gang used to go looking for him to beat him up. They did not like that Ramon took Margarita from one of their own. He also tells how he finally won her over and, two years later, married her.

It was one hot summer morning when I was going to school with a terrible hangover. I had been drinking till 3:00 AM on a Sunday night dance in Guadalupe, Arizona. Guadalupe is an Indian settlement south of Tempe, Arizona, about five miles distance. This was on my last year of junior high school. I had been attending Tempe Grammar School since kindergarten as a small boy. This was an all-white school that prior to a lawsuit against discrimination against Mexican, Indian, black, and Chinese, only whites could attend that school. Tempe Eighth Street School was for the Mexicans. This was the school that Margarita attended. The person or, I should say, Mexican who filed a Class Action lawsuit against the Tempe Grammar School and won the lawsuit case was named Mr. Romo. I went to school with his children and I also had the pleasure of meeting him. He was a very nice person. At that time, the whites used to call us Mexicans and they really enjoyed it. They treated us like we were from Mexico, not Native-born Americans. I used to walk from my house on West First Street to school. I say that the school was about three miles from our house. I used to walk on the railroad tracks because it was shorter distance. This Monday morning, I'm walking for no apparent reason, I get off the tracks on East Eighth Street toward Mill Avenue. As I walked to Mill Avenue, I came in view of the Mexican school (Tempe Eighth Street School). I saw some of my friends going to school there, friends that I grew up with. They asked, "What brings you over here?" At that time, I really didn't know why I had taken that route to school. Then I saw this beautiful girl across the street holding a school patrol sign. I couldn't keep my eyes off of her. Then I turned to this friend of mine, who was the person in charge of the School Safety Patrol (Charlie Acedo). I asked him, "Charlie, who is that girl across the street?" He answered me that she's Marjorie Perea, Charlie Perea's sister. I fell in love the moment I saw her and I crossed the street in order to get a better view of her. As I pass by her, she knew what I was up too. She pretended not to notice me, but I also knew she was looking at me to find out who I was. She also hadn't seen me around town. I felt sort of shaky on my legs. I really felt something deep inside of me. I felt like I had never felt before. I suppose one can really say that I fell in love with this girl. One can say that it was love at first sight on my part.

I was fifteen and a half years of age and on my last year of junior high school. School was going to be out in three months and I knew deep inside of me that this girl was going to be my wife. Oh, yes, I played the field with girls, but I never felt this way. As I write my family history, this beautiful and gorgeous girl has been my wife for fifty-nine years and has bore me six beautiful children, three boys and three girls. Now they have their families growing up. This girl changed my life for the better. She has always been there for me. She came from good Christian stock. She was and still is a member of the Church of Jesus Christ of Latter-day Saints, commonly known as a Mormon, and so am I since 1954. Her father and mother knew my parents' way before I was born. They used to dance to my father and brother's music in the towns of Morenci, Globe, Safford, Superior, and Miami, Arizona. When Margarita and I started to go steady, her mother found out that our stepmother did not feed us. When I would visit Margarita at her father's house, her mother would call into the kitchen and sit me down on the table and bring me a plate full of food and tortillas. It was during this time when I was courting Margarita that I started to have problems with the Pachuco gang of Mesa, Arizona; her former boyfriend was a member of that gang. They would go over to Tempe just to see if they would see me somewhere alone.

They could never get me alone because I was always with someone of our gang. Then one Saturday night, a dance was going to be held at the college's B. B. Moeur Building, some of us had been drinking out of town. There was a dance in Tempe. The dance was being held at the B. B. Moeur Building. When we got to the dance, the music had already started. Margaret was already dancing with him and I waited for him to go to the restroom. He hadn't seen me yet. As he opened the door and went into the restroom, I told the guys that were with me, "Don't let anyone in until I take care of business." They knew that I was going to mix it up with Gilley, that was the guy's name. As I stepped into the restroom, he looked at me surprised. We had a few words and then he threw a punch at me. He hit me on my shoulder and I said to him "Is this the best you can do?" And I let him have it on the jaw and he went down. I didn't let him get up. I kick him all over. I picked him up and stuck his head in one of the commodes. He said "You're a better man than I am, let me go and I won't bother Margarita anymore." So I let him go and he went back to his hometown in

Mesa, Arizona. That made things worse for me. The guys from Mesa really got mad for what I had done to one of their gang members. They would look for me every weekend. They were hoping to find me somewhere in Mesa or Guadalupe. All the time that they would find me, I was with the guys from Phoenix or Tempe, but never alone. One weekend, one of my so-called buddies invited me to Mesa to the dance. I told him that Margarita wasn't going to the dance that night. He said we'll go just to see what is going on at the dance then we can come home and drink some beer with the guys. I remember very well, that as the bus that went to Mesa passed by Margarita's house, she was sitting on the front of the house. I saw her there and me though to myself, she saw me going to Mesa, now I'm in for it. Margarita never did see me on the bus going toward Mesa. When Ruben and I got out of the bus and started to the Melendez dance hall, we talked about our girlfriends because at that time he was going around with Mary, Margarita's sister. He told me how much he loved her and I said to him, "If we love them, then what the hell are we doing here?" He said, if you do as a woman will tell you not to do this or that before getting married, when you get married, they become the bosses of the house and you have to follow their orders and you are no longer the man of the house. I said to him, married couples are supposed to work together and to do what we are doing isn't right.

As we paid to go in, we ran into Margarita's former boyfriend and another Mesa gang member. They told Ruben, "What the hell, are you guys doing here?" And before we could answer the question, this other guy hit Ruben in the ear and he started to bleed and he took off running. I said to myself, "What am I doing here standing and not helping Ruben?" So I took off running after them. I caught up with both of them, because they were running after my friend Ruben. I caught them by the shoulder and they stopped. I told them," Leave him alone. He isn't looking for trouble." Then the same guy told me, "You want the same thing that I did to your friend?" I said, "Yes, if you're man enough." That was the moment that Giley, Margaret's ex-boyfriend, hit me on the right side of my head and the other guy came at me hitting me in the face and nose and I started to bleed. Then I went after Giley and punched him all over his face and stomach and he went down. Then I started to kick him in the ribs and he said, "No more. Don't hit me no more." And I told him, "Get up, you yellow belly." But he didn't get up, he stayed on the ground.

Then this other guy came after me, throwing punches at me and I blocked most of them, and then I went after his stomach, hitting him left and right until he went down for the count. By that time, all of their gang had gotten behind me and started to throw punches and kicks at me. There were about nine of them and I tried to mix with all of them, but they were too many to fight and what I did is I went under a car and they started to throw rocks at me. Good thing that the police came over and chased them away. I was all bloody of so many punches I took from the gang. What really got me mad was that Ruben never came to help me. I saw him standing on the other side of the street. He came over to me after every thing was over and said to me, "You sure gave them a run for their money." And I grabbed him by the shirt and said, "Don't you ever call me your friend. You're nothing but a coward." I never again hanged around with him.

Chapter 37

In this chapter, Ramon reveals the change that his father took to him for revealing what he saw Mage was doing with other men. His father used to beat him up with his belt and belt buckle and later with the horsewhip for telling on Mage. He was fifteen years old when he told his father that he wasn't going to be whipped by him anymore.

Before closing my part of my history, let me state that I didn't have the best of having a normal teenager's life at all. I began to be mistreated by my stepmother and my own father about the age of ten. Margarita, whom we called Mage for short, was very mean from the very beginning she started working for the family as a housekeeper. After she had been with us for a year, she moved into our house with her two daughters, named Dahlia and Dora Louisa, and Gilbert, her little boy, whom I nicknamed Coily because he had his head full of curls. That nickname stayed with him for the rest of his life. The girls were already teenagers and they were all very nice to us. That is, Josie, my little sister, and my bigger brother Fito. We noticed right away that Mage was feeding her children better than us. She would give them more food on the plates and seconds if they wanted more, but not us. Mage would serve us our food on the plate with one tortilla and a fork and a spoon and if we asked for seconds, she would come right out and tell us that the rest of the food was for her and dad. Yet if one of her own children would ask for more servings, she would serve them more and just walk away from the kitchen.

Mage had this for us, if she called us for supper and we didn't show up till later, we did not get fed and we had to go to bed without eating anything. This is about the time that I got smart and I went around the neighborhood to visit my friends about the time they were going to eat supper. I knew that both fathers and mothers would invite me to eat with them. I played it smart and didn't go there every day. I used to go to a different house the next day. They knew what was going on at our house with Mage. Sometimes they would tell me, "Go, get your sister Fina (short for Josephina) so she can eat with us also, but don't let Mage know nothing. If she asks you two where you're going, just tell her you're going over to play with my children." The families that made sure we ate some food before going home were the Alvarez family and the Rivas family. I used to eat quite often with the Alvarez family. I believe that they wanted me to get married with their daughter. I saw her as being a sister to me, not a girlfriend. She married eventually two years after I got married. She married a nice man who is still with her to this date.

Mage started to make supper around seven or eight at night after she got through sweeping outside of the house. I have to say this about her. She was a very clean person on house cleaning. I believe that Mage took a bit of hate toward me because she wanted us to call her mother and I told her right out that she wasn't our mother and would never be. After this, she started to give me house chores that were woman's work. She would have me do the beds, sweep the inside of the house, wash the family dirty clothes, iron the shirts and pants, wash dishes, and dry them and put them away. She would also put me to set the table for the family to eat, even though she hadn't cooked anything yet. In plain words, she had me doing all this as a punishment for not calling her mother. She started to tell my father that I was very mean with her. When she told me to do any kind of housework, Father believed her what she would say about me and then Father would take the belt off and spank me in front of her. When Father spanked you, you better not cover your butt with your hands. Father would hit you until you took your hands from behind you. As I grew up, he would no longer whip me with his belt. He would use his horsewhip instead and hit me on the butt and my back. This reminded me of the white slave owners of the South who would hit their slaves who were disobedient to orders in the plantations of the South. He would hit me as if I wasn't his son. Later as I grew up to the age of fourteen, Father had a belt buckle with a violin on the center of it. He was very proud of the belt buckle. It was awarded to him by the Musicians Union of the WPA (Workman's Program Act). He played violin with this orchestra during the depression years. He was considered a skill journeyman at that time. I remember so well the day that he was going to whip me with the horsewhip and couldn't find it. He took his belt off and was going to hit me with the belt buckle again and as he swung it at me, I, in some way, was able to grab the belt buckle as it came at me and I grabbed it and yanked it out of Father's hand. I threw it on the ground and looked at him and said, "This is the last time you're hitting me. You're not going to hit me no more. I'm growing up and it's a disgrace to me to be beaten up by you as big as I am."

He looked at me, turned around, and walked off and never said a word to me, and from that day, I was never beaten again. In spite of what Mage would say to him, Father didn't pay attention to her. This is the time that she left me alone. She never again said anything to my father again about me. But prior to these, I used to go to school with purple belt bruises on my hands, arms, and back. My schoolteacher used to ask me, "Ramon what happened to you, why do you have all those bruises." I would answer her, "I got them playing football at home." I don't believe that she swallowed the stories or excuses that I came up with. Almost forgot to say that the day that father couldn't find his horsewhip was that my sister Fina (Josephine) hid the horsewhip. One of my main reasons that I used to tell father what Mage was doing was that one day after school, some of my friends went over to play hide and go seek. This is a game that one person has to go looking for someone and if he finds him he has to tag him, but the game isn't over until he finds everyone playing and the one that he tagged first becomes the person that has to find the kids playing the game. This game can go for hours playing it.

Chapter 38

Ramon tells why he feels that his stepmother mistreated him more than the rest of his brothers and sisters. He had always been truthful to his father, yet his father did not believed him on the things he saw with his own eyes and Mage knew that he was telling the truth.

I didn't like Mage for not telling my father the truth that there were times that I caught her with other men making out. Father would approach her after I had told him what I saw. She would deny that I saw her at all. Father without waning would turn around and hit me with whatever he had in his hands or anything close to him. The last time he hit me was the time that I took the belt away from him. This was because I told him that I caught Mage and Tony Alcantar having sex in one of the railroad cars about half a mile from the house. When I got home, my father asked, "Ramon! You didn't happen to see Mage in town?" I responded, "No, but I did see her with Tony Alcantar having sex in this boxcar." He said, "Don't lie to me." And I told him, "Father, I'm not lying to you now or the other times before. I have never lied to you because I knew you would punish me if I did and you found out the truth later." I told father what I saw and he didn't say a word. He turned around and went inside of the house and waited till Mage got home. Father called me and in front of Mage he asked, "Ramon, what did you tell me about Mage and Tony Alcantar?" I related to both of them what I had seen Mage and Toni doing in the boxcar. Mage got very mad and started calling me a liar. She knew that I saw her and Toni because she started hollering at me not to tell my father. I did tell my father what I saw. I should have known better by now who father was going to believe. He took his belt off and started to hit me. I remember that I got mad and I took the belt out of his hand and threw it on the ground and I said to my father, "This is the last time you're going to hit me with the belt or any other thing you want to hit me with. You have whipped me for the last time and you will no longer hear me tell you of Mage's doings. I have been telling you the truth about her and you have never believed me and you always take her side." Funny thing that I recall is that others in the neighborhood had told my father the same thing I had told him all this years and got whipped for it. I wondered all this years why father believed her instead of me, his own son. I finally put it together after all these years being married. Father was not yet married to Mage, but was having sex with her and this way he continued to have sex with her in showing her that he was on her side. I sure paid a price for him to have enjoyment in his life.

Chapter 39

Ramon talks about how all this affected his life as a grown man and what he has gone through. After many years, he still remembers like it was yesterday when all this happened to him. He talks about his wife's mother who loved him like her own son. Ramon expresses his true feelings about her.

What has been hard for me is that those memories are still part of my life. Writing the family history for my family has been a very emotional thing for me. It brings the past of my youth into focus and I see that I'm lucky to have met my wife and her family early in my life. We met at the age of fifteen and her mother and father talk to me like as if I was their own son. They taught me how to be a gentleman, what to do and what not to do. They hugged me and kissed me on my forehead or cheek. They taught me how to love and show that love to people. They were the ones that taught me of what I am today. I call my mom "Mom." Her name is Maria Hernandez Perea. To me she was my real mother here on this earth. She knew my real mother here on this earth also. I believe that they were very close sisters before coming here to this earth. Sometimes, I think in this way. My natural mother must have told Mom (Maria), "I'm going to give birth to this son, but I'm going to have to leave this earth we're going. But I want you to take good care of Ramon. He is going to need someone like you to help him develop into a good man. He will probably marry one of your daughters and become a son to you." This is the thought that comes to my mind sometimes when I think about them both. I love Mother Maria with all my heart and soul.

I miss her and think about her often. I pray that when my time comes to leave this earth, she will be the one to meet me after I go through the veil into the next world, take me to my natural mother, and tell her, "Rita, this is your grown son Ramon." And she will respond, "Thank you, Maria, for taking good care of him. He grew up to be a good man. Thanks to you and Gonzalo. Now he has two mothers to love him and enjoy him forever." This is what I hoped happened when they met in the spirit world. They all have passed away into paradise where all spirits of God's children go to wait for the resurrection. Writing this family history has been a strain on me. Because as I remember certain events that happened to me. I get very emotional inside of me remembering how bad I was treated as a teenager in my own home. I tell you, it's hard during this time that I have been doing research on our family tree members.

Chapter 40

Ramon found out that his own brother and his son swindle the Chavarria families out of their savings. He thought that he was the only one until one of his sisters died and the family got together after the burial.

I have come to find out that we have had two family members that have swindled money from certain family members, including me, by not letting each one of us know what was going on. Roberto and his son Robert Jay developed a scheme how to swindle each one of us, out of thousands of dollars. They made each one of us feel sorry for them by telling us a story of how their business partners would cancel their business deals on putting Robert Jay's inventions to work. They showed us papers and documents of what their business would look like and the place of business buildings. All this scheming was done by telling us how they lost all their money because the partners would cancel their deal with them. We found out that the papers they showed each one of us were false. In plain words, they played us for suckers and got our money. They got $4,500 from me. They were supposed to have paid me in three months and it's been eleven years that they haven't even send me a penny.

They have also lied to the other members of the family. Some have been waiting to be paid by them for over twelve years and still haven't received a penny. Roberto and his son are very deceitful, liars, and thieves in my book. I filed a conspiracy against them and I had to stop because my attorneys told me that I also had to file against Molly, Roberto's wife, because she was the one that received the money on her check account. She is completely innocent of the whole matter. Poor Molly, they both lied to her about the money. Well now, she knows about it and the family isn't happy about what they did to the families, we have all broken our family relations with them. We know that we will never get our money back. It's a lesson well learned. Never feel sorry for a family member whom you don't trust. Have them sign an agreement by law. We all didn't do it with them. We might as well forget in being paid. They don't have any money to pay rent, let alone pay us. They will pay someway here or beyond the grave

Chapter 41

Ramon gets the surprise of his life by a phone call from his brother Tony. Tony tells him how he and his stepdaughter Paula found the documents hidden inside of one of the closets that father built. Ramon tells him to send him the documents. Ramon finds that some of the documents are fraudulent. He also notices that the signatures of his father and uncle are also fraudulent.

I also worked for General Dynamics Convair Division in 1990 to 1993. On a very nice day in March 1994, I received a surprise of my life. Tony, my little brother, whom I visited every year in Tempe, Arizona, and brought each other up to date on family affairs calls me and says, "Are you standing up or sitting down?" I responded, "I'm sitting down. Why?"

"Brother, you won't believe this. We found a homestead land certificate in Dad's old home that is going to be demolished by the City of Tempe. We might be the owners of this land. It seems that the land is around Laveen, Arizona, a few miles from Phoenix." He said to me, "Brother, of all the family members, you are the only one I can trust on this." This is how I got involved helping my brother Tony. He related to me, why he didn't trust the rest. "You, brother, have always been truthful with everybody you know. I don't want the family involved yet. We will tell them if this certificate is still good." This happened in the year 1993 on August. This is the way he told me out of his own mouth, how him and Paula, his stepdaughter, found the land certificate.

Tony was invited by Rose Montanez, who happened to be Gilbert's (Coily) ex-wife. Gilbert is the person that bought our father's property. Before his death, we, the family, always thought that the property on 520 West First Street, Tempe, was our fathers, but it wasn't. The land belongs to the State of Arizona. The houses on the property were the only ones that belong to Father. Later the State notified all those residents that wanted to buy the land could do so. Our father didn't have the money to buy the land, so he asked Gilbert if he wanted to buy it, Gilbert did buy it and he let our father live on the property until his death in 1973. Parts of our father's children were not notified about buying the land for us or Dad. Only the older brothers knew about it. I wasn't notified about buying the land. I found out about it seven years after. Gilbert was our father's stepson. Also Gilbert was the one that took care of our father in his later years. He also drove him around to the store or doctor's. He deserved it. He did take good care of our father and besides our father took Gilbert at the age of seven. Gilbert was like his own son.

The purpose of Rose calling Tony was to see if he wanted anything out of the house before the City demolished the house. Father had some old pictures and furniture that used to belong to our mother (Rita) for souvenirs and some other stuff our father had saved all these years. The City had condemned the old house because the neighbors had complained that it was a hazardous firetrap and that drug addicts and homeless persons were using the house as a haven to sell drugs and the homeless to sleep at night. The house became vacated after our father's death in 1973. Gilbert did not fix it or take care of it. He locked it up and almost forgot about the house. The reason he didn't do anything to it was that he knew that the City of Tempe wanted all that properties for the expansion of the Salt River recreation area. The City did buy the property from Gilbert. Tony and his stepdaughter Paula went to the house and when they arrived there, Gilbert's sons and daughter were there already ransacking the house. They took a lot of stuff that really belong to us. Later I found out that they sold it to a secondhand store. What Tony did was to tell Paula that he was more interested on a light green fishing tackle box because our father kept his violin belt buckle in that fishing box under lock and key, he also carried the key in his wallet and that he wanted that buckle.

We, as his children, knew that father kept all his important papers and the belt buckle in that fishing box. Tony knew about the belt buckle because he was the last of the family sons to stay with father and he also saw father take the belt buckle out and clean it. That is why he was interested in the belt buckle. It was a nice-looking buckle. Father kept all his important papers and the belt buckle in that fishing box under lock and key always. Nobody went into that box unless father opened it and he got whatever papers you wanted to see. When they search for family paraphernalia that day, Paula, Tony's stepdaughter, found the box in the bedroom closet behind a stack of old clothing that had spoiled with the rains. Tony quietly whispered, "Take it to the truck and don't let them see you with it, they might want the fishing box." My brother Tony told me that the reason he whispered to Paula was that he was afraid that Gilbert's family might want what was inside the box, and take the belt buckle and sell it. Paula was very careful not to let them know what she had found. When Tony and Paula arrived at home, Tony's wife, Betty, and daughter Paula went through the contents of the fish and tackle box and found an old leather pouch with some paper documents inside of it; also in that pouch was a government brown envelope and a homestead land document belonging to Francisco Chavarria in 1895. This happens to be our father's father, our grandfather. The document was a land given to United States citizens who wanted to settle in certain areas and farm. The document was signed by President Grover Cleveland on April 15, 1896. We are the sons of Pablo Chavarria, who was the second son of Francisco Chavarria Sr. The homestead document states that this land is located in Solomon, Arizona. In 1876, Solomon was known as El Pueblo Viego (Old Town), named by the Spaniards in 1540. This strip of land is on both sides of the Gila River.

This land is to be in the possession of Francisco Chavarria heirs, to have and to hold the said track of land forever. The homestead document was filed on 9 of May at 9:00 AM 1896 by Eugene Trippy (county register) at Tucson, Arizona, Bureau of Land Management. This document is recorded at Safford Arizona, Graham County. The land certificate was filed for record on 26 of May at 5:00 PM, and recorded in book six on pages 303-304 at the request of Mr. Blas Ortiz, who was grandmother's husband since the death of our grandfather Francisco Chavarria in 1890. They got married in 1893 in Solomonville, Arizona. Blas Ortiz used to be a farmhand for Grandfather Francisco. Blas was also an Indian. After their marriage, they never had any children. The person who recorded the certificate for Blas Ortiz was Mr. Manuel Leon (county recorder). The homestead certificate is recorded at the land office. Volume 2, page 129 and is signed by a Mr. M. McKee and Mr. L. S. C. Lanair, recorder of the General Land Office, Tucson, Arizona.

Our brother Tony also found some other documents, one such document is a land mortgage loan on the land. The mortgage loan papers state that Francisco Jr. and Pablo Chavarria borrowed $174 from Mrs. Mashbir, who owned a real estate agency in Safford, Arizona, and the 136 plus ninety-four hundreds of an acre was the security on the loan, including the water rights on the land stated on water certificate # 622 of the Montezuma Canal, known today as the San Simon River. This small river runs right through our grandfather's land. Grandfather bought 6 1/2 percent of all the water that runs on it. All this water runs into the Gila River into the San Carlos Lake. This loan of $174 on the land is signed by both brothers, Francisco and Pablo Chavarria. I asked Tony to send me copies of all the papers that he found including the original land document. I told Tony that I wanted to have them check for forgeries. Also I wanted to see for myself what we were looking for.

Tony sent me copies of everything they found on the metal box. He sends me the original land certificate. Telling me to send it back after I had shown it to the congressman (Republican Duncan Hunter). When I received the packet, the land document was inside a government brown envelope. I took the homestead certificate and had it copied by a friend of mine that works for Kinko copying company in San Diego, California. It was copied like the original in color. One cannot tell if it's a copy or not. After showing the original to the congressman who offered to help me get the land back, I mailed it to Tony, since he was the one that found it. (This was a mistake in my part, sending it back to him.) I should have kept it in my possession. This will be coming out in what happened to that homestead certificate. If I would have known what was going to happen, I would have kept it. After studying the documents, I called my brother Tony to discuss the papers in the fishing tackle box where they found all of father's important papers. I asked my brother, "Tony, are you sure you found this entire document in the fishing box of father?"

He got very upset with me on the phone for doubting him about the discovery of the homestead certificate and the rest of the documents. That's when I told him that I was familiar with the contents of the fishing tackle box. I told him about the birth certificates of the family that father kept inside of that box and also that I did our fathers taxes every year and we always took everything out of that box to get the information we needed to file the tax forms. I told Tony that I had never seen those documents he was telling me about, which he sent to me. He then said maybe our father had them hid somewhere else. I didn't want to get into an argument with my brother. Then I said maybe he did and decided to take them out and put them in the fishing box. How our brother Tony got those documents will be coming out later.

The loan papers did have some signatures that looked like his and Uncle Francisco's. I had never seen uncle's signature so I really didn't know if it was his signature. Then I remembered that I had in my possession our father's signature and Uncle Francisco's on father's delayed birth certificate. Knowing our father's signature and Uncle's, I said to Tony, "Tony, those signatures are not father's and Uncle Frank." He then said to me, "Brother, how can you prove that statement?" I said, "I have our father's signature on his delayed birth certificate from the Virgin De Guadalupe Catholic Church in Solomon, Arizona. Father had to apply for his birth certificate in 1942 to register for the draft. Uncle Francisco was his witness that he was born in Solomonville, Arizona, in 1882. Uncle Francisco also had to sign his name on the baptism certificate." I also told Tony that the signatures on the Mashbir loan papers were fraudulent also. I mentioned to Tony, "Brother, someone in the family had to forge those two names. The signatures look almost like the signatures of our father and Uncle Francisco."

"Why don't you call the Bureau of Land Management in Safford and find out if the land certificate is still valid? It might be that time has run out on it to claim the land." In the meantime, I did some research on the documents and found out that the signatures were false (fraudulent). Tony did call the land office and gave them the numbers on the homestead land certificate. They told him that the certificate was still good and that the land was in Solomon, Arizona, not Laveen, Arizona, and that the land was occupied by some people farming it. I also found out that according to records on Father and Uncle Francisco, the signatures on the loan papers had to be someone who knew about the land and forge the brother's signatures because one brother was not of age (Pablo) to sign land documents. The loan papers state that both brothers are twenty-one years of age. "Not true." Uncle Francisco was, but not Pablo. The loan papers show that the name Chavarria is misspelled. One signature has a *b* instead of a *v*. It also has one *r* instead of two *r*'s. The name Chavarria is misspelled like this: Chabaria. Also both brothers never wrote in the Old English writing. Both names are written in the English lettering. That is the fancy way of writing business letters, if one is properly educated in the Old English lettering. Both brothers were educated up to the fourth grades. Both brothers knew how to read and write. This will come up later how I'm able to prove all these documents with their signatures are fraudulent. As I continued to do research on the family land case, I found how other people got involved on the fraud. The statement given by Mr. Charles L. Rawlins (notary public) on February 9, 1884, is false. Our father Pablo Sr. was born on January 25, 1884, at Solomonville, Arizona, Graham County. Somebody else had to sign those loan papers of Mrs. Mashbir. Later on investigation of family history, I received some church baptisms from the Catholic Church in Tucson showing that our Father Pablo was really born on March 25, 1882, not 1884. That really did make him to be twenty-one years old and could sign on such documents, but it wasn't him that signed or Uncle Francisco.

Chapter 42

This chapter deals with the water rights. Tony finds out that the land is still under the name of Francisco Chavarria.

At this time of the land investigation, none in the family really knows that he was born in 1882 instead of 1884. Tony and I figured that our father wasn't old enough to sign those loan papers. Because Francisco and Pablo would have had to show proper identification that they were the individuals signing for the loan on the land and as owners of it and also the water rights on certificate #622 of the Montezuma Canal of 9% ownership of all the water that goes through on that canal to Mrs. Mashbir. On March 20, 1994, at 7:00, Tony called me and told me that he called the Phoenix land office of the Bureau of Land Management for the information on the homestead document; I gave him instructions what to ask for. The land office referred him to call the Bureau of Land Management in Safford, Arizona. Tony related to them his concern about the homestead document. He gave them the number of the land document and they went to the record book, and they found the information on the land. As far as the record books indicated, the land was under the name of Francisco Chavarria. That if there had been a mortgage on the land, no record of it was on the Bureau of Land Management. "If there had been a loan on the land, the two brothers must have paid it off." (The land office mentioned to Tony that if the loan had not been paid off it would be on record at the land office, still under the name of Mrs. Mashbir.)

They also mentioned to Tony that if his father, the last of the heirs to his father's estate, paid the mortgage off, he would not have the document on the homestead in his possession. Tony was advised to file a land status report. The report would show the original owner and who would be the present owner today. It would also show if the land still belonged to Francisco Chavarria. The information given to Tony was that if we had the original homestead certificate in our possession, that we, the Chavarrias, would be the legal owners of that land. The land is located in Solomon, Arizona. Part of the land is located up north from the center of the Gila River and due south from the Gila River to the town of Solomon, Arizona. With this information at hand, I told my brother Tony that we would need the help of Arizona Senator John McCain who is a member of the Bureau of Indian Affairs Office in Washington, D.C. I went to see my congressman, Duncan Hunter, who I know personally. I took the original homestead certificate to him to see it. He looked at it, checked the signature of the President Grover Cleveland. After viewing the certificate, he looked at me and said, "Ray, go to Safford, Arizona, and walk into the Bureau of Land Management Office and tell them you're here to claim your father's land that belonged to your father. Show them the homestead land document and proof that you are Pablo Chavarria's son and that you're claiming the land in behalf of you family."

He also called the Bureau of Land Management in Safford. I was sitting in his office when he did this. He identified himself and the land office gave him the same information as they did us, that the land was still on their books and computer, showing that Francisco Chavarria as the legal owner of the land and more information that they had provided us with. I was hearing all the conversation on the congressman's loudspeaker phone in his office. The woman that was on the phone with the congressman mentioned to him that the U.S. government had taken twenty-two million out of our land in 1906 during the depression to help pay the expense of the war.

Mr. Cato Cedillo, Congressman Hunters's executive administration assistant, myself, and the congressman were present. I could not believe what we heard. Later on, these were documents sent to us from the Washington National Archives during my investigation of the land document. One must remember that my purpose to go see the congressman was to see if he could help me get an appointment to go to see Senator John McCain in Phoenix, Arizona.

When Tony and I met with Senator McCain's staff members in his office in Phoenix, we brought with us the original homestead document to show the senator that we had the original, making us the owners of that land in Solomon, Arizona. We made the presentation describing how the document was found by Tony and Paula, his daughter. We left copies of all the papers we had in hand and gave them some questions to get answers to each one by the Bureau of Indian Affairs and the Department of the Interior. After a few days, Tony called the Safford Consolidated Realty in Safford concerning the title search they were to send us. Mr. Burk was very rude with Tony this time and told Tony that the status report was not mailed to us because there was no land under the name of Francisco Chavarria in 1896.

Our brother Tony then asked Mr. Burk what had made him change his mind when before he told him that the land was under the name of Francisco Chavarria. Mr. Burk told Tony that our father Pablo and his brother Francisco Chavarria had sold the land to a Mrs. E. S. Mashbir in

1904. He said that he was going to send Tony the $128 back. Mr. Burk said there was no documentation on the books on the sale of the land. That it seemed to him that we are committing fraud in claiming the land that doesn't belong to the Chavarrias anymore and that we have no case to pursue. Then Tony told him that the loan papers that showed that our father Pablo and Uncle Francisco signed in Feb. 9, 1904, are not their signatures. These signatures are fraudulent. This is when our brother told Mr. Burk that whoever signed those loan papers committed fraud, not us.

Mr. Burk responded that in those years (1800), any recorder of documents was authorized to sign the names of persons doing any transactions with them (notary public). That is the reason the signatures of our father and uncle were not their own. Tony told Mr. Burk that the statement he had just made was false. He told him if a person did not know how to sign his name, he or she would sign with an x witnessed by someone else to make it legal. Then Mr. Burk gave Tony his own opinion concerning the matter at hand. He told Tony that our uncle and our father were trying to borrow money on land that they no longer had in their possession. That to him, they were the ones committing land fraud.

Tony mentioned to Mr. Burk that the signatures on the land mortgage loan was fraudulent. Mr. Burk got very upset at Tony's line of question. He then told Tony that there was no record on such land loan, that he was not going to send us the status report. Mr. Burk states that, as a matter of fact, there is no record of any transaction on this land. We figured that he knew more on this land than he gave us information on. He was very adamant and said, "If you want to see the land title, go see Mr. Claridge. He is the legal owner of this land." Then he hung up on our brother Tony. A month later, our attorney received the status report from Consolidated Realty showing how the land was swindled from the Chavarria family by the State of Arizona. Remember that the documents that showed the two brothers signing were fraudulent signatures. Then we started to receive through the mail copies of all the transactions on the land through the offices of Senator John McCain and Congressman Duncan Hunter, both members of the Republican Party. We received copies of all the recorded land documents. How our great-grandfather became the owner of 2,400 acres of land through the Treaty of Guadalupe Hidalgo of 1848. This treaty took the upper north land from the Gila River then in 1853, the Gadsden Treaty Purchase gave him the south part of his land and he and his family became United States citizens.

When we received the homestead application from the Bureau of Land Management Tucson, Arizona, Tony and I studied the documents and we saw the start of the land conspiracy. The trip that our grandfather took in 1890 to Tucson was to submit his land application for an Indian Trust

Homestead Patent. Grandfather made the application on U.S. Codification 2289 section outside of the reservations to have as much rights as Indians inside of reservations to allotted lands of 160 acres per adult Indians. Here is where we started to find out what our father had told me at the hospital.

That is father was Indian and also his mother. His father and his grandfather were born in Warm Springs, New Mexico before Arizona was a Territory in 1848-1853. Through the 1860 Federal Census of New Mexico, we found that our great-grandfather was Francisco one of the chiefs of the Warm Springs Apaches, later known as the Coyoteros. Francisco's Indian name was (El Fresco) and he was a friend of Cochise, Mangas Coloradas, Nana and other Great Indian Chiefs. He was in the battle of Apaches Pass in 1863 with Cochise. They went in raiding parties with Cochise into Mexico. In Mexico they raided cattle and horses and took Mexican women and children as captives to sell in the towns of Arizona as slaves, in order to buy guns, ammunition, and whiskey.

Our great-grandfather Francisco (El Fresco) covered the areas of Globe, Aravaipa, Redington, Tucson, Tubac, Tombstone, Duncan, Sierra Bonita (Graham Mountain), San Carlos, Camp Goodwin, Fort Thomas, Thatcher, Safford, Solomonville, Bisbee, Morenci, White Mountains, and Dos Cabezas mountain. In 1864, Francisco had a disagreement with Cochise concerning the innocent killing of the white women and children. As an Indian Chief, he claimed the land from Safford to Solomonville on both sides of the Gila River. Solomonville was named at that time El Pueblo Viejo by the Spaniards in 1545. The treaty of Guadalupe Hidalgo of 1848 gave the land to great-grandfather including U.S. citizenship and his family.

Great-grandfather Francisco, being a White Mountain Apache chief, was entitled to a small part of the land that his band of Indians roamed. He chose the land on both sides of the Gila River known at that time as the silver strip. He became domesticated and a cultivator of the soil. He was tired of the Indian wars and in 1865, he and his family marched from their home of Pueblo Viejo (present-day Solomon, Arizona) and turned themselves in to the U.S. Cavalry at Camp Goodwin. They took him as a prisoner of war because he was with Cochise at Apache Pass. They let the rest of the family go free. His son Francisco, who later became our father (Pablo), was with him when they all turned themselves in at Camp Goodwin about six miles from Fort Thomas. Great-grandfather was mistreated at the Camp Goodwin. He tried to escape from this abuse and in 1865, he was shot by some of the U.S. Cavalry guards in the back while he was running to escape from the camp.

This is the time that our grandfather started to ride with Cochise, Geronimo, Mangas, Juh, Loco, Nana and Victorio, Taza, Natchez, and others. Grandfather Francisco went on Indian raids to Mexico below the border to towns like Janos, Bavispe, Corralitos and the surrounding areas of Sorora and Chihuahaua, Mexico. According to the stories told by our grandfather to my older brothers and sisters, after the year 1873, the United States took our grandfather's land into the San Carlos Indian Reservation. They stayed on their land inside the reservation. Then seven and a half years later, it was removed out of the reservation to become a public domain land.

Our grandfather had to apply for his land as a homestead patent land, even though the United States government had granted that portion of land to our great-grandfather in 1848 through the Treaty of Guadalupe Hidalgo and the right of becoming a United States citizen. The upper north portion of his land from the Gila River came under the Treaty of Friendship. Then in 1853, the Gadsden Treaty Purchase took the bottom south portion from the Gila River. This is what the United States government did to swindle the land from our family, making it a public domain land in 1873. Even grandfather's constitutional rights were violated by the federal government.

I wonder, why did grandfather have to make application for a Homestead Patent land? This land was his already. Why did the land in general stay unoccupied by Mormon settlers? This was, and still is, prime land. Was it because the family was still living in the land after the freak horse accident of our grandfather in 1891 a few months after he applied for his homestead? We must remember that no one in the family knew that Grandfather Francisco had made application for the land he and the family were living all this time since great-grandfather owned it. This must have been preemption land in the beginning; that is why no settler took it as a homestead land.

They found out that the Chavarrias owned that property in the first place. This is why the silent conspiracy took place after the death of our grandfather. In 1895, Grandmother Refugia had to go to the land office in Tucson, Arizona. The purpose of that trip was to go and file the necessary papers on the land. These were the final proof papers on the land. Grandmother had been already married to Blas Ortiz since 1892. Grandmother was no longer the widow of Francisco Chavarria. The only heirs to the land were Francisco Jr. and Pablo Chavarria. Both sons were underage at this time. This is where Blas Ortiz found out that the land was not going to his wife Refugia, but to her two sons. Blas Ortiz found out and that he would not be the owner of this land also. He must have told his drinking buddies, namely Regino, our grandfather's own brother who was an alcoholic, who was always getting into trouble and getting locked up in jail.

Jesus Sainz, who was grandfather's son-in-law, and also his wagon master when Grandfather Francisco was alive, was a very mean man and a very conniving person. My father told me Jesus was about 230 pounds, six feet tall and was an expert on the rifle. He banged around the town drunks as a constable in Solomonville when he wasn't working for grandfather as wagon master. Jesus did not have any pity for the women of ill repute that worked in the little bar in Solomonville to entertain the cowboys coming to town to have a good time. He would bang them against the wall, kick them, and punch them in their body as if they were men.

Manuel Leon worked at the County land office. He handled the recording of the land deeds going to different persons around the surrounding areas in Pima County, later Graham County. These four persons, Blas Ortiz, Regino, Jesus Sainz, and Manuel Leon, were drinking buddies. Blas Ortiz must have mentioned the homestead land to them during one of their binges. Regino Chavarria got into some very serious trouble with the law. Uncle Regino was going to go to prison. His lawyer was E. S. Mashbir. Mashbir and his wife also had a real estates office in Safford, Arizona. (The county seat of Graham County in 1904.)

Regino made a deal with Mr. Mashbir to get the land of his nephews in a scheme of fraud. Regino and the Mashbirs plotted to swindle the land away from the Chavarrias in drafting a loan of $174 plus the water rights to the land certificate No-622 of the Montezuma Canal (San Simon River) in 1904. The Mashbirs faked the signatures of Francisco Jr. and Pablo Chavarria. But before they could carry their plan of fraud, Regino was promised money and freedom from prison. He told his drinking buddies what the plan was and promised each one so much money to keep quiet. In the meantime, Blas Ortiz and Manuel Leon kept quiet concerning the homestead certificate that had come to the heirs of Francisco Chavarria, his two sons Francisco and Pablo Chavarria. Blas Ortiz kept the homestead document hidden from Regino and the rest of the drinking buddies.

Let me take the history back in order that it may be better understood how I was able to obtain all of this information. On 23 of April, I called my brother Tony to ask him some questions concerning our grandfather, Francisco Chavarria. The reason I needed this information was to find out which of the Franciscos was on the land certificate, our grandfather or his son. I also wanted to find out when our grandfather had died. Tony told me that he was going to get in touch with Paul and Ralph and ask them when grandfather died. The answers from our brothers were that our grandfather was born in Chihauhaua, Mexico, and he died in 1891 on a freak horse accident. The land in question was Grandfather's and our uncle Regino's. The land belonged to both of them. Let me mention at this time, none of our brothers and sisters never even knew that a homestead certificate was in existence. They all believed at this time that after the death of our grandfather that the land went to his brother Regino.

They told Tony that grandfather and his brother Tio Regino inherited the land from their father (Great-grandfather Francisco) and that great-grandfather had no last name. Grandfather was baptized by Jesuit priests in Three Rivers, New Mexico, and given the name of Francisco Chavarria. They also told him that the Indians used to visit grandfather in Solomonville. That Geronimo, Natchez, and Taza used to come with Geronimo and stay at his ranch before going on raids into Mexico. They mentioned to Tony that Grandmother Refugia related to them this account in 1920. Grandmother passed away in 1928 at the age of 80.

After Tony told me this information, I called our brother Ralph and asked him what had happened to the land certificate. He said, "Monchie, there was never a land certificate on the land. Grandfather never had a certificate on the land. If our father would have known or had in his possession such a document, he would have told me and showed me the document." He also told me that when I moved to California, he took my place in doing all his paper work, such as Federal Income Tax Insurance papers and other things. Then I asked him, "Ralph did you ever see any land papers in father's fishing tackle box where he kept all of his important paper?"

"No, why?" he asked me. At this time, I felt it was not the time to tell him what Tony had found at the old house. I said, "Brother, I'll let you know why I asked you these questions. I have to make sure of certain things that are happening concerning the land grandfather owned at one time." Ralph said, "The land belonged to Tio Regino after grandfather died. He sold it to some Mormons in 1904. That's when they had to get out of the ranch. Tio Regino sold the land and built a saloon in town and had women of ill repute working for him at the saloon. Tio Regino used to go to Mexico and bring young girls to work for him. Some would marry and leave the place and he would go back into Mexico and bring some more."

This is the time that I was sure that the brothers and sisters did not have any idea about the homestead deed. Since our grandfather died in 1891 and the homestead certificate came to the Chavarrias in 1895, it had to go back to the Bureau of Land Management in Tucson, Arizona because the bureau told us that they had made a mistake in the names on the certificate. They say that the names of Francisco heirs were on the certificate. The names of Francisco Jr. and Pablo. The certificate had to have the name of the entry person who would be our grandfather Francisco Chavarria on it, not the heirs. The homestead certificate came back in 1896. We asked the Bureau of Land Management in Tucson, Arizona, to send us a copy of the original homestead patent. We wanted to see the mistake that was made and the correction made.

This came after I received the copies of the application of our grandfather Francisco in 1890 and the final entry of grandmother in behalf of her sons, Francisco Jr. and Pablo, our father. I noticed in grandfather's application that he did not know how to write his name. He signed with an *x* witnessed by the clerk filing the land application. I noticed also that Grandfather filed under Codification 2289 section 15. I went to the law library in San Diego, California to see what this code 2289 section 15 stood for. The Indian law book stated that Codification 2289 section 15 was the law that covered Indians filing for homestead patents under the Dawes Act of 1887. This Act included that Indians who made application on public domain lands.

The Indian had the same protection under the law as any Indians in reservations who had allotted lands of 160 acres. This Act (the Dawes Act) gave this same Indians that the Bureau of Land Management would protect their land for twenty-five years or more. Then I also found out that in 1934, the government did away with allotted land inside of reservation patents under the guardianship of the federal government. The government would continue to take care of their lands under the guardianship of the law permanently. If an Indian wished to sell their land, they had to have the authorization from the Bureau of Land Management.

This is when I wrote the Bureau of Land Management in Tucson to send me a copy of the first homestead patent that came to the Chavarria heirs. I believed that the first homestead document was an Indian Trust Patent under the guardianship of the government and that the land was preemption land. Preemption land means that the person has been residing on that land before making application for homestead land under the Indian General Homestead Act of 1886, known as the Dawes Act. This Act of Pre-exemption was for Indians only. They were free from having to pay taxes on that land as long as they owned it. Once it was sold by permission of the Bureau of Land Management, the land was taken out of trust from the government and taxes would have to be paid by the new owners.

I found out through federal documents sent to me from the archives in Washington, D.C. including the Bureau of the Interior and the Indian Affairs Office that the government took the land out of trust and the State of Arizona passed it on in an Adverse Action Court Order in 1952 to E. M. Claridge. The family was not present to claim the land. Simply because none of us knew anything concerning the land as ours. We didn't find out until 1990 when our brother found the homestead document and the mortgage papers of the loan of $174. After getting all the documents on the land, I had a private hand expert who has his business here in Chula Vista, California. He retired from the FBI in Washington, D.C. as a handwriting expert for the government.

I sent him some of my father's handwriting and our uncle Francisco's from the early 1900s to 1972. He matched the handwriting on the Mashbir loan mortgage papers and found the signatures on the loan papers to be fraudulent signatures on those papers. That meant that our father and his brother did not know they were the true owners of all the land and that Tio (Uncle Regino) claimed to own after the death of his brother Francisco Chavarria. I called the office of Congressman Duncan Hunter and told Mr. Cato Cedillo that Mr. Burk from the Consolidated Realty Office in Safford had refused to send us the status report. I mentioned to Mr. Cedillo that Mr. Burke told us that there was no information on the land in the books concerning the sale of the land.

I asked Mr. Cedillo if he could call Mr. Burke and ask him if he could send us the status report that we had paid his agency for. Mr. Burke at this time had not sent Tony the $128 back. Mr. Cedillo from the congressman's office called me the following day to tell me that he did talk with Mr. Burke and he related to me the contents of the conversation between them. Mr. Burke had done a small investigation on the land lease sale of my uncle Francisco and my father. There was no need of a status report. Mr. Cedillo explained to me all of what Mr. Burke had told him on the phone. After my conversation with Mr. Cedillo, I called Tony and related to him what Mr. Burke explained to him what he had done. Mr. Burke found no evidence of irregularities on the sale of the land.

After our conversation, I asked Tony to call the land Recorders Office in Safford and tell them to send him all they have documented on the sale of the land and we will pay for all the copies and mailing expenses. After he received it, send it to me so that I could study all the documentation and see for myself if there were any discrepancies and in case there was that I could make the Office of the Congressman aware of those infractions. On April 25, 1994, at 11:30 AM, Tony called me and said that he called the Recorders Office in Safford and that the lady that answered the phone was very polite and very cooperative in helping him get whatever information he needed.

The lady in the Recorder's Office told Tony that the computer and the log books show no Francisco Chavarria of having any land whatsoever. And to top it all, that no Francisco Chavarria ever existed on record. I said to Tony, "This is unlawful to tamper with State documents." On March 4, 1994, prior to Tony's phone call to Safford, I received a letter from that Office of the Recorder from the person in charge, Ms. Shirley Angle. She stated, "At the present, it seems that the property belongs to the Claridge family. If the legal description is correct. Just looking through the index of Grantors, Francisco Chavarria sold several parcels. I do not know if this is the right one."

We found out later that these were the parcels of land that Tio Regino was selling when grandfather went on his hauling ore trips that took him weeks away from home. Also, when the land was lost in 1951 on the adverse action in Safford Courthouse, all the people on that judgment paper were the people that bought the parcels of land from Tio Regino. Tio Regino falsified his brother's name, Francisco Chavarria, on the land documents. This is why when the land was lost in 1952 in Safford, none of those people could prove they own their lands. They lost also and that is the reason that the Claridges have so much land today. This land sold by Regino was part of the 2,400 acres of land that Great-grandfather left his son Francisco, our fathers' father, for an inheritance in 1865.

I began on an in-depth back history of the Chavarrias and Sainzes. Our Tia Carmen married Jesus Sainz. Jesus was involved in this conspiracy with the others involved of the family including Tia Carmen. I came across some documents in the Safford Courthouse that the land that belonged to the heirs of the Chavarrias, Francisco and Pablo, was divided in the year 1899 (another false document). I hired a surveyor to survey the land on the Mashbir mortgage loan including the Safford land papers that show this removal of the gold out of the land and the names of the mining companies that took part in mining the gold on grandfather's land in 1899.

The survey company that I hired to do this work of surveying the land documents is DGB Survey & Mapping, 837 East J Street, Chula Vista, CA 91910. This is their report after the survey.

October 11, 1995

Dear Mr. Chavarria,

In response to your request of my review of certain documents, the following is my interpretation of the parcels of land as described in the Probate Decree dated July 25, 1899, of the Probate Court of Graham County in the Territory of Arizona and the current configuration of those parcels today.

Refugio Ortiz received a parcel of land containing 68.5, the point of beginning being the center of section 13, Township 7 South, Range 26 East, Gila & Salt River Meridian; Thence West, along the center of said section, 1,320 feet; Thence North to the South bank of the Gila River; This distance would then be 2,260.5 feet by using the acreage divided by the distance of 1,320 feet. Each of the parcels received by Francisco Chavarria, Pablo Chavarria, and Carmen C. De Sainz were 22.85 acres each and contiguous to the above-described parcel and to each as they run westerly 440 feet each and northerly to the south bank by using the acreage divided by the distance of 440 feet. If this being the case, the Gila River would have to be running in a due East-West direction.

The general Legal Description of lot 2, Section 12 and lot 6 and 8 and the South Half of the Northwest Quarter of Section 13 in Township 7 South, Range 26 East, Gila and Salt River Meridian, and those parcels as described above, are those parcels that lie Southerly of the Gila River, that the Northerly parcels lines of these parcels terminate in the South bank of Gila River and the Southerly parcels terminate in the South bank of the Gila River and the Southerly parcel line being the East/West centerline of said section 13.

In summation, these parcels are those parcels of land lying within the Southwest Quarter of Section 12 and the Northwest Quarter of Section 13 below the Southerly bank of the Gila River.

Sincerely,
Donald G. Baker, PLS

The document that had the information that the land was first divided among the family was in 1899. This was another fraudulent scheme to get the land away from the Chavarrias. Tio Regino was the person behind this scheme to get money for his drinking habit. Regino, with the help of Tia Carmen and Jesus, convinced grandmother to give Regino her part of the land and he would share the money he would get for the land with her. She believed all of them and gave the land that belonged to her to Regino. He sold the land to a family by the name of Gilliland who later sold it to the Galespies who abandoned the land in 1932. This is the time that different mining companies came into the land and took the gold that was underground.

Then in the late thirties, the Claridges squatted the land, filed for a wild deed, then a quiet deed, then in 1951, they filed an adverse action against the Chavarrias and the other people that bought land from Regino, and won the land. Try to remember that this is Arizona law that was applied to this case. Now here comes the interesting part. The homestead certificate #717 application 1459, recorded vol. 2, page 129. This document is signed by the President of the United States Grover Cleveland in April 15, 1896. This land is an Indian Trust Patent under the guardianship of the federal government. By law, this land belongs to the heirs of the last Chavarria. We are the sons of that person. Pablo Chavarria was the last heir to the

Homestead Trust Patent. We are his heirs and entitled to this land. Only a court of law can determine who is the legal owner of the land. And the only way we can prove ownership is through our Indian Trust Patent issued to our grandfather in 1896 by the government of the United States. The Congress of the United States is going to get involved because they are the body that made those laws of legal ownership to Indians. At this time, January 18, 1998, all the documents on the land case have been turned over to our attorneys, Vllassis & Vllassis of Phoenix, Arizona. George Vlassis is working with the Congressman Duncan Hunter to find the proper procedures by law in handling this matter.

Although we have uncovered many documents to prove who started the silent conspiracy of stealing the homestead land of our grandfather from his heirs, we have also found out that some of the family members were involved. As I mentioned before, all our older brothers and sisters who came to be Father's first children by his first marriage to Dolores Amado Chavarria all believed that the land belonged to Great-uncle Rejino. That after the death of his brother (Grandfather Francisco Chavarria), the land went to his brother Regino and that he had the right to do with it as he pleased. But we found out by research that he was the main character in the swindle of the land from his nephews, Francisco and Pablo Chavarria, the truthful heirs of the land.

You have to realize that Grandmother Refugia did not know how to read and write. I uncovered this on her homestead final proof land application. Grandmother signed with an *x* witnessed by Manuel Orta. I've also seen that when grandfather made the application to his homestead land that he also signed with an *x*. I asked all of my brothers and sisters if they knew if both grandfather and grandmother knew how to read and write. They responded that they did not know if they did. When I told them that they did not know how to read and write, they did not believe me until I showed them the land application on the land including the homestead certificate. They could not believe their eyes. They were so surprised at seeing the documents. They asked me a hundred questions, "Where did you find all this information? Who had it? What did they intend to do with it? Who found it? Why did they do this to the family?"

This is when I told them the truth. That Tony, our younger brother, had found it at the family's old house in father's old fish and tackle box. Two of my brothers said to me, "Monchie, that is not true what Tony told you. He stole that document from our father's metal box before he went into the U.S. Navy in 1951." Ralph told me, "Brother, I used to do our fathers income tax and I used to go through that box every year and I never saw those documents. I did notice a leather pouch that father never took out that used to belong to Blas Ortiz. Father kept Blas's belongings, especially that metal box." Ralph said to me that he gave our father the fishing metal box and an Indian leather pouch that Blas Ortiz carried around his waist and never permitted anyone to see it. Father loved Blas Ortiz as his father and had a great respect for him that he never opened that pouch to see what was inside. Ralph was the one in the family that went looking for Blas when he didn't come home for lunch. He went to the water canal behind the property of Ed Bertalsen and found Blas Ortiz dead. This is what he said to me: "The last time I went through father's metal box was in 1951 and the leather pouch was not there anymore." He did not press the issue because Dad never said anything pertaining to the pouch.

Then I told my brother Ralph, "After you quit filing father's income taxes in 1951 I took over and I never saw the leather pouch. So we figured that our brother Tony took it out of the metal box and had it with him during his navy hitch of twenty years." Why would our brother do such a thing to the family? One may ask. I understood our brother Tony. Tony was taken away from the family when our mother Rita passed away in 1937. Tony was about two years old when Aunt Ramona, mother's sister, took Tony to live with her in Wilcox, Arizona. He did not come back to us until he was fifteen years old. When he came back, all of us had gotten married and had children already. Tony never grew close to us to build a tight bond with us.

And to top it, all he brought with him was two hundred dollars from Wilcox. He gave it to our father to save it for him. When he wanted to buy parts for his bicycle, he'd ask our father for some of his money. Our father told him that he had used it for buying food for the family. Our brother got very angry with our father for using his money without his consent. After a few days, Tony made a false withdrawal slip at the post office where father had his savings. The postmaster Mr. Ed Miller saw the slip that Tony used to withdraw some money for his bike and he told our father, and he got a hold of Tony at the house and was going to whip Tony. It just happened that I arrived at Father's house to visit him. This is when I saw my brother Tony take the belt away from Father.

Tony was very angry at father that he went after father and I got him by the shoulder and turned him around and gave him a hard slap on the right cheek that he almost fell on his knees. I told Tony why I had to slap him and that's when he told me why he had done what he did to our father. I remember telling Tony that he had to respect our father. Yes, he had a right to question father about his money but not to hit him. That alone I told him shows lack of respect to one's father. After my brother Tony came home, he told me that he had forgiven me for slapping him when he was arguing with father. But to the rest of the family, he told them he would never forgive me and that someday he would get even with me for slapping him. I have found out that our brother was a good liar. He could look at you straight in the eye and lie to you, and make it so convincing as the truth. When I told Tony that I never saw the homestead document in father's metal box, Tony looked at me angrily and said to me, "Are you calling me a liar?" I didn't want to argue with him. I said, "Forget it." And that was the first and last time that I brought that up again. Roberto asked the same question to him at Tony's house at Tempe, Arizona. He responded the same way he did to me. So we all forgot to question him again. We all came to the conclusion that Tony took the certificate from Dad's metal box before going into the navy.

Tony passed away in Sept. 4, 1997, of a heart attack. At his funeral, I met a friend of his. He was a very tall Native American of Apache ancestry. He was a participant in our brother's funeral. He had an Indian burial ceremony. After the services, I thanked him for helping the family with the services. This is what he told me: "I have known your brother when he moved from Bellflower, California. In 1976 after your father's death, I started to help Tony in trying to get some land back that was in Solomon, Arizona. He had in his possession a federal homestead certificate." I asked him, "Are you sure this was in 1976 when you were trying to help him?" He looked at me and said, "Ray, I am a medicine man in my tribe. I don't make false statements to people."

"We couldn't find any information so we quit in 1982. That's when he told that he had a brother named Ray who might be able to help him with the land search. A few days before his death, we had lunch and brought me up-to-date." He then said to me, "If anyone can get that land for him, it's my brother Ray." Let me say this. Tony had told the family that he had two sons in his first marriage to Ruby. Then he married his second wife Betty who was with a child when he met her in a bar in Long Beach, California. They named the child Paula. Then he calls me in 1994 to tell me that he had a son by one of the daughters of a family friend. The boy was named Robert "Bobby" Rivas.

At Tony's funeral, the family met for the first time all of Tony's children. He had nine children, three girls and six boys. Our brother had lied to the family concerning all of his children, plus the homestead patent certificate. I'll say this concerning our brother Tony. He took after our great-uncle Regino. He was a liar, cheat, womanizer, alcoholic, and a bragger. After the funeral, two weeks later, our oldest sister (Refugia) passed away. The family met at Corral's Mexican Restaurant in Scottsdale, Arizona. This is what all of my brothers and sisters revealed to me. These are the family's past dark secrets they had kept in the closets. They never wanted to reveal them to us who were the sons and daughter of Rita, father's second wife. Betty, our oldest sister, after the death of Refugia (Cuca), starts the conversation by saying to me, "Ramon, since you are tracing our family roots, you might find that in our family there was a killing of one of our cousins. He was shot by his father. Remember this happened many years ago when our father was twenty-one years of age (1905). Our Tia Carmen got married to Jesus Sainz in 1889. Jesus Sainz was a widow. His wife died leaving him with a young son. His name was Gabriel Sainz. When our aunt married Jesus, Gabriel was seventeen years of age. Gabriel was a very handsome boy. Somewhere both our aunt and Gabriel got involved in a love affair. Nobody in the ranch or the town of Solomonville knew what was going on between the two."

Since Jesus was our grandfather's wagon master on grandfather's freight wagon, they would be gone for six weeks at a time. They would deliver the cargo to towns all around Solomonville. "Ramon, in these years, men had to work in whatever they could get a job. Our grandfather was a very hard worker. This was told to us by his wife, our grandmother. She is the one that told all of us what happened in this love affair between her daughter Carmen and Gabriel." Then Lolita took over the conversation. "This love affair started after Jesus and Tia Carmen got married. Aunt Carmen was seven years older then Gabriel. Tia Carmen was around twenty-one and Jesus Sainz was forty-five years of age when they got married."

Lolita and the rest of the family believed that since Jesus was much older than our tia, that our tia must have fallen in love with her stepson. When Jesus and grandfather would go on their hauling trips, Tia Carmen and Gabriel were left alone at the ranch for weeks at a time. Both were very young to be left alone at the ranch. Even though they lived at the Big Ranch. Jesus, Tia Carmen, and Gabriel lived in a separate house about a block away from the family's main house. Then all hell broke loose. Someone saw Gabriel and our aunt holding hands and kissing downtown of Solomonville. Rumors started to travel around the town of what was going on at the Sainz house. Jesus was unaware of all this at this time. He was on the road with our grandfather.

When Jesus Sainz came home, he went drinking with his drinking buddies, Regino Chavarria, Blas Ortiz, and Manuel Leon. They drank all night and during the night, Jesus Sainz got in an argument with someone over a hand in poker. This person revealed to Jesus that the town was talking about his wife and son. That his wife was nothing but a whore. Jesus beat the daylights out of this person. This is sometime in the morning around nine. Jesus got on his horse and headed for the ranch. Somebody or friend of Gabriel warned him that his father knows of his affair with his wife and that he planned to kill him. Gabriel got some clothes, got on a wagon, and started out of the ranch.

As Gabriel neared the school, he saw his father with his rifle on his hand. He got scared because his father is heading toward him on his horse. Jesus starts to holler to his son about his sneaky love affair with his wife. Gabriel jumps off the wagon and runs toward the school fence. As he climbs the fence and was about to jump to get away, Jesus raised his Winchester rifle and shot his son clear through the stomach. Jesus was a marksman with the rifle. When Gabriel hit the ground, he was dead already. Jesus was tried for murder of his son. What saved him is that Aunt Carmen testified in court that in the morning of the shooting, Gabriel came into her bedroom and tried to rape her.

While they were struggling in the bedroom, Jesus came into the bedroom, saw his son trying to rape his wife, and went to her rescue. Gabriel, being much younger than his father, knocked him down and got on top of him to hit him with a branding iron. Aunt Carmen picked up her husbands gun from the floor and shoots Gabriel in the stomach and he dies. They did not believe her story about the shooting of Gabriel. Betty said, "He went free because of the law those days. If a man found his wife in bed or otherwise having sex, the husband had all the rights of the law to kill both of them." This is the way they believed it happened as told by our grandmother to them.

The killing, according to Court records happened in February 14, 1908. This is a print of the INDICTMENT against JESUS SAINZ.

IN THE District Court

of the fifth District of the Territory of Arizona, in and for
the County of Graham
April Term. A.D. 1908

TERRITORY of ARIZONA
            VS   INDICTMENT
    Jesus Sainz

——————————————————— Jesus Sainz ———————————————————

is accused by the Grand Jury of the County of Graham, Territory of Arizona, duly empaneled and sworn, by this indictment, found this 23rd day of April A.D. 1908 of the crime of _____ MURDER _____ committed as follows; The said JESUS SAINZ on or about the 14th day of February A.D. 1908 and before the finding of this indictment, at the County of Graham, Territory of Arizona, willfully, unlawfully, feloniously, deliberately, premeditatedly, and of his malice aforethought, in and upon one Gabriel

Sainz, a human being, an assault did make, with a certain gun, then and there loaded with gun powder and leaden bullets, and by him the said Jesus Sainz had and held in both hands, and with said gun loaded as aforesaid he the said Jesus Sainz then and wilfully, unlawfully, feloniously, and with deliberately premeditated malice aforethought, did shoot the said Gabriel Sainz, then, thereby wilfully, unlawfully, feloniously and with deliberately premeditated malic aforethought inflicting in and upon the body of said Gabriel one mortal wound, of which said mortal would the said Gabriel Sainz then and there did die. And so the said Jesus Sainz, did, in the manner and form aforesaid wilfully, unlawfully, feloniously and of his deliberately premeditated malice aforethought, kill and murder him the said Gabriel Sainz, a human being.

Contrary to the statutes in such case made and provided and against the peace and dignity of the Territory of Arizona,

L. N. Shatton
District Attorney

These are the people who were summoned by the Court to give evidence in the case pending between the Territory of Arizona as plaintiff, against Jesus Sainz:

Miguel Rojas, Jaruis Soto, Juana Perea, Francisco Chavarria, Pablo Chavarria, Valentine Arduso, Alfonzo Luna.

This is an excerpt from the actual trial transcript of Jesus Sainz dated February 24, 1908.

L. S. BECTON, WITNESS.

District Attorney:

Q. What is your name?
A. L. S. Becton.
Q. Where do you live Mr. Becton?
A. On the Big Ranch.
Q. What is your business or occupation?
A. Working on the Ranch.
Q. Do you know Jesus Sainz, the defendant here?
A. Yes, sir.
Q. Did you know Gabriel Sainz in his lifetime?
A. No.
Q. Did you know a young fellow that worked on Olney's ranch?
A. Yes, sir.
Q. What was his name?
A. I don't know.
Q. When was he killed and where was he killed?
A. He was killed up here in front of the school house.
Q. Who killed him?
A. This man over here, the defendant.
Q. Was you there?
A. Yes, I was there.
Q. Will you state what occurred there between the defendant and the boy that was killed?
A. He was there, this big man. When I saw him he was off of his horse and the man that got killed was getting off of the hay, and when I seen them again this fellow that shot him he was going around the wagon.
Q. Then what occurred?
A. He run up and down that way about five or six times before he shot.
Q. What was the boy doing?
A. He had his six-shooter in his hand?
Q. Could you see the position that the deceased was in in regard to the pistol?
A. He had his pistol in his hand chasing up and down beside of the wagon, bearing away from the wagon, away from this big man, and when he had beared off a good little piece from the side of the

wagon this defendant shot him down through under the back of the wagon. Then after he shot him down the big man run around the wagon and jumped on him and went to hammering him with something, I don't know what it was, and when he got up from there he had a six-shooter in his hand.

Q. Whose six-shooter?

A. The Boy's six-shooter.

Q. What did he do then?

A. Then he got up on his horse and rode off with his six-shooter in his right hand. That's all I saw.

Q. Now, you said he was hammering him, what do you mean by that?

A. He jumped on him and hammered him with something, I don't know what it was.

Q. When did you first see the pistol?

A. When he raised up from him.

Q. When did you first see the defendant?

A. When this one hollered whoa, it was the first time I seen him. He was off of his horse.

Q. Where did you boys come from that day?

A. We come from the Big Ranch.

Q. And where did you go?

A. We went to the Depot.

Q. When you got your hay weighed where did you go?

A. We went around the corner towards the School-house.

Q. Where were you when you first saw the defendant?

A. I saw him on the ground.

Q. Where were the wagons at that time?

A. Right in front of the School house.

Q. Did you hear any conversation between the defendant and deceased?

A. They were saying something in Spanish, but I did not understand what they were saying. I don't understand Spanish.

Q. In what position was the deceased when the big man got on him?

A. He was down.

Q. In what position was the boy that was shot, how was he lying?

A. He was laying with his head South-like.

Q. Was he on his back?

A. Kindly face foremost.

Q. Where was his hands, before him or to the side of him?

A. I don't know what position they were in.

Q.   Was his face towards the wagon or in another direction?
A.   Towards the wagon, I believe.
Q.   Did you see the defendant when he fired the shot?
A.   Yes, sir, I was looking right at him.
Q.   In what position was the boy when the shot was fired?
A.   He was stooping down under the wagon.
Q.   Was he facing the big man, the defendant?
A.   Just as he started to shoot. I don't know whether he wheeled when he shot or not.
Q.   What did the deceased do with his hands at that time?
A.   The six-shooter was in his hand in that position (witness showing position), kindly down over him when I seen him.
Q.   Was the defendant on the ground prior to the time when the deceased got off the wagon?
A.   He was on the ground when I saw him.
Q.   Where was the deceased when you saw him?
A.   He was on the left of the wagon.
Q.   Where was the dead boy?
A.   He was coming off the load of hay.
Q.   Was the defendant on the ground prior to the time the deceased got off the wagon?
A.   Yes.
Q.   Did you see the deceased point the pistol at the time, at any time?
A.   I did not.
Q.   Were you looking at him most of the time?
A.   Yes, most of the time while they were chasing up and down the wagon.
Q.   At the time the defendant fired the shot, did the deceased have his pistol at that time pointed in the direction of the defendant?
A.   No, he didn't have it pointed at all.
Q.   Do you know whether or not he ever cocked his pistol?
A.   No, sir.
Q.   How far was you from the man that got shot?
A.   I was on one side of the road and was standing by the mules heads when the gun was fired.
Q.   About how many yards were you from where he fell?
A.   I don't know, sir.
Q.   Just make an estimate?
A.   I was not more than five or six yards from where he fell.
Q.   Was that in this County and Territory?
A.   Yes, sir, in Graham County, Arizona.

Cross-Examination.

McFarland:

Q.   You were driving the second wagon?

A.   Yes, sir, the hind wagon.

Q.   And the deceased was driving the first wagon?

A.   Yes, sir, ahead of me.

Q.   Were the wagons pretty close together from the scales to the point where the difficulty occurred?

A.   Yes, sir.

Q.   When the wagon stopped at the place where the difficulty occurred, how far were the leaders on your wagon from the rear end of the front wagon?

A.   About 15 or 20 feet.

Q.   From the heads of the leaders of your wagon?

A.   It was not over 8 or 10 feet.

Q.   How many people were present there at that time except yourself, the deceased and the defendant?

A.   I don't know, sir.

Q.   Was there any person except you three?

A.   There was a lady on the sidewalk close there.

Q.   There was no others at the road except you three?

A.   No, sir, not at that time.

Q.   How far up, in reference to the first wagon, did the defendant ride before he got off of his horse?

A.   I don't know.

Q.   Had he gone by the front wagon before he got off his horse?

A.   No, just about the rear end of the front wagon.

Q.   When you saw him got off of his horse, and turned around to look at the driver of this wagon, he was off of his wagon wasn't he?

A.   The deceased was just about off of his wagon as defendant got off of his horse.

Q.   What distance would it be from the ground to the top of this hay where deceased was riding?

A.   It was six bales high of hay on top of the wagon.

Q.   About how high is a bale of hay?

A.   About one foot.

Q.   Then it would be six feet from the top of the wagon to the top of the hay.

A.   Yes.

Q.   Then about four feet to the ground?

A.   Yes, sir, about four feet.

Q.   Then, when you looked over and saw the defendant getting off of his horse the deceased was getting down off the hay?

A.   This man, the big man, was there and down before the deceased got off the wagon.

Q.   You say they were having a conversation?

A.   Yes, sir, they were talking in Spanish.

Q.   Did you know the deceased had a gun before that time?

A.   Yes, sir, he has been packing it all the time since he has been working on the Big Ranch.

Q.   When you first saw him on the ground after he got off the hay, did he have the pistol in his hand?

A.   Yes, he had the pistol in his hand.

Q.   And had the pistol in his hand until the fatal shot was fired?

A.   Yes, he had it in his hand until he fell.

Q.   Did you see the pistol in the hands of the deceased before he reached the ground?

A.   No, Sir, I did not see it in his hand until he reached the ground

Q.   You did not see him take it off of any part of his person

A.   Just as soon as he hit the ground he had the pistol in his hand.

Q.   He might have had it in his hand before, so far as you know?

A.   I don't know, that was the first time I saw it.

Q.   Which side of the wagon did the deceased get down on?

A.   On the right hand side.

Q.   That would be this side?

A.   Yes, sir

Q.   You say the deceased was not in plain view of you all the time?

A.   No, sir.

Q.   Was that because your mules were in the way of the front wagon?

A.   It was because I was ahead.

Q.   You say you did not see him all the time?

A.   I was sitting behind the wagon that the deceased drove.

Q.   Then when you got by the house where he was his wagon would obstruct the view?

A.   Yes, sir.

Q.   Did you hear the deceased say anything at the time the wagon stopped?

A.   They were talking something or other, but I could not understand what they were talking about.

Q.   Did you hear him say anything to his team?

A.   He said whoa, as he slided off of the wagon.

Q. Where was the defendant at the time he was sliding off of the hay?

A. He was on the side of the wagon near his horse.

Q. Then the defendant had not started over towards the wagon at the time deceased slided off the hay?

A. No, Sir.

Q. Did you say that the defendant was at the rear of the front wagon?

A. Kindly at the back end and the deceased was kindly to the front end, to the right.

Q. You could not see him very well sliding down on the opposite side?

A. I don't guess I could.

Q. Did the defendant go over towards the wagons until after there had been more or less conversation between the deceased and defendant?

A. Yes, sir, they were saying something or other before the defendant started over towards the wagon.

Q. But you did not know what that conversation was?

A. No, sir, I don't understand Spanish.

Q. Was that conversation before or after the deceased got off of the wagon?

A. It was after he got off of the wagon.

Q. Well, there was no conversation between them before?

A. They were saying something all the time before they were down.

Q. Was there any conversation between the deceased and defendant before the deceased got down off of the hay?

A. I could not tell whether there was or not.

Q. But there might have been a conversation before the deceased got off of the wagon?

A. There might have been, I didn't hear any.

Q. Were you occupied at something at that time?

A. Yes, sir, I could not hear them.

Q. Now, was the defendant on his horse the first time you saw him?

A. He was off of his horse when I saw him.

Q. Were the wagons stopped at the time you first saw the defendant?

A. Yes, sir.

Q. Both stopped?

A. Yes, sir.

Q. And you say that the defendant (I allude to this man here when I say defendant) with the horse was standing just about opposite the hind wagon when the deceased got off of it, and that the wagons were stopped at that time?

A. Yes, sir.

Q.   Did you see the defendant when he first got off of his horse?
A.   Yes, sir.
Q.   He was off of his horse when you first saw him?
A.   Yes, sir.
Q.   When you turned your eyes from the defendant to the deceased, who was on the first wagon, was he sliding down on the said of the hay.
A.   Yes.
Q.   Then the defendant, when he got off of his horse, would have been behind the deceased, wouldn't he?
A.   He was next to the hind wheel of the second wagon.
Q.   Close to the wagon or off some distance?
A.   He was about 4 or 5 feet.
Q.   He would be in the road as well as the wagons, wouldn't he?
A.   Kindly on the slope of the road.
Q.   In order to get by the wagons he would have to get on the slope, wouldn't he?
A.   I don't know.
Q.   He was there the first time you saw him?
A.   I don't know.
Q.   He might have been further up towards the front end of the first wagon?
A.   I don't know.
Q.   He might have been?
A.   I don't know, sir.
Q.   He was not further up than the rear of the first wagon?
     (No answer)

RE-DIRECT EXAMINATION.

Q.   Which one of the wagons do you call the first wagon?
A.   It was the head wagon.
Q.   Who was driving that one?
A.   The boy that got killed.
Q.   Well, now, where was the defendant's horse?
A.   He was standing down at the hind wheels of the wagon.
Q.   What was the distance between the horse and defendant when you first saw him?
A.   About 5 or 6 feet.
Q.   Did you hear any conversation or any words spoken at all prior to the time he got off of the wagon?
A.   No, sir, I did not hear anything.

Q.   How much of a conversation did they have during the time they were on the ground?

A.   They were talking all the time.

Q.   Were there any people immediately behind the defendant on the East side of the wagon?

A.   There was one lady?

Q.   How far was she from the defendant and what direction?

A.   She was kindly down to the left of the wagon.

Q.   Did you see the school children as you passed by?

A.   I did not notice.

TERRITORY OF ARIZONA,   )
)   SS.
COUNTY OF GRAHAM.   )

I, the undersigned, Cullen A. Little, having been duly appointed by Justice of the Peace, A. H. Austen, as Reporter to take the evidence in the Preliminary hearing of the case of the Territory of Arizona vs. Jesus Sainz, held before said justice in the Justice's Court of Precinct No. 5, Graham County, Territory of Arizona on the 17th day of February, 1908, do hereby certify that the foregoing is a correct statement and transcript of the testimony given before said Court on the 17th day of February, 1908.

Cullen A. Little

Subscribed and sworn to before me this *21* day of February, 1908. My commission expires *April 23, 1911.*

B. J. Kellner
Notary Public in and for Gila
County, Territory of Arizona

(4—405 a.)

THE UNITED STATES OF AMERICA,

To all to whom these presents shall come, Greeting:

Homestead Certificate No. _717_

Application _1459_

Whereas There has been deposited in the GENERAL LAND OFFICE of the United States a CERTIFICATE OF THE REGISTER of the LAND OFFICE at _Tucson, Arizona Territory_ whereby it appears that, pursuant to the Act of Congress approved 20th May, 1862, "To secure Homesteads to Actual Settlers on the Public Domain," and the acts supplemental thereto, the claim of _Francisco Chavarria_ has been established and duly consummated, in conformity to law, for the _lot numbered two of Section twelve, and the lots numbered six and eight and the South half of the North West quarter of Section thirteen, in Township seven South, of Range twenty six East of Gila and Salt Lake Meridian, in Arizona Territory, containing one hundred and thirty six acres and ninety four hundredths of an acre_

according to the OFFICIAL PLAT of the Survey of the said Land, returned to the GENERAL LAND OFFICE by the SURVEYOR GENERAL:

Now know ye, That there is, therefore, granted by the United States unto the said _Francisco Chavarria_ the tract of Land above described: To have and to hold the said tract of Land, with the appurtenances thereof, unto the said _Francisco Chavarria_ and to _her_ heirs and assigns forever; subject to any vested and accrued water rights for mining, agricultural, manufacturing, or other purposes, and rights to ditches and reservoirs used in connection with such water rights as may be recognized and acknowledged by the local customs, laws, and decisions of courts, and also subject to the right of the proprietor of a vein or lode to extract and remove his ore therefrom, should the same be found to penetrate or intersect the premises hereby granted, as provided by law. And there is reserved from the lands hereby granted, a right of way thereon for ditches or canals constructed by the authority of the United States.

In testimony whereof, I, _Grover Cleveland_, PRESIDENT OF THE UNITED STATES OF AMERICA, have caused these letters to be made Patent, and the seal of the GENERAL LAND OFFICE to be hereunto affixed.

GIVEN under my hand, at the City of WASHINGTON, the _fifteenth_ day of _April_, in the year of our Lord one thousand eight hundred and _ninety six_, and of the Independence of the United States the one hundred and _twentieth_.

BY THE PRESIDENT: _Grover Cleveland_

By _M. McKean_, _Secretary._

Recorded Vol ___ Page ___

Our father Pablo never said anything concerning the shooting of Gabriel. But we heard him several times having arguments with his sister in Tempe and Phoenix accusing her of being at fault for the killing of Gabriel. This is what the family had hidden all these years from us. Then in August 15, 1997, the Chavarria and the Sainz families had a family reunion at Solomon (Solomonville), Arizona. I used this trip to gather information for our family history. I figured that if they tried Jesus Sainz in Safford Courthouse, they might have the records there. Since the wife and I stayed at the new Ramada Inn in Safford, Arizona, six miles from Solomon, Arizona, I made a visit to the old courthouse in Safford.

When I approached the courthouse, I felt the spirit of humbleness. I stopped and asked the Lord to guide me to find the truth on the shooting of our cousin Gabriel. As I went up the stairs, I looked all around and said to myself, "This is the place where Tio Jesus was tried for murder of his son." I felt that I had gone to the past. That I was actually walking up the same steps that my ancestors walked to the trial of one of our own family members. When I went into the courthouse, I found nothing but workers refurbishing all the rooms inside the courthouse. A very nice gentleman asked me, "Can I help you?" I told him that I was looking for the County Recorders Office, and that I had come all the way from San Diego, California, to a family reunion in Solomon and that this was the area of my ancestors. I asked if I could see the courtroom where they held the trials in the 1800s. He said, "Of course." He said to me, "Can I ask why you want to see that trial room?" I answered him, "Of course, you can."

"Why do you want to see that part only?"

I responded, "One of my uncles was tried here for killing his son late in the 1800s."

"What was his name?" he asked, "if I'm not asking out of order."

I said, "His name was Jesus Sainz."

Then he said, "One of his granddaughters is working here as an elected official for the County of Graham. You're walking on thin ice on this search." I asked him why. He said, "Two years ago, the Safford News published the trial of Jesus Sainz and the whole family wanted to sue the newspaper here in Safford."

After our conversation, he took me to the trial courtroom where Uncle Jesus was tried. I felt sorry for both of them, the son for getting killed for lack of respect toward his father's wife and the father for taking the life of his own son. I wondered in that room if he felt any compassion toward his son. Did Jesus stop to think what was the right thing to do? Or did he let his bad attitude take over his whole body to commit murder of his own son? The gentleman that showed me the place also told me that all the offices of the court were located on the basement of the courthouse. Then I approached the area of the county recorder.

Here I was standing in the same room that my family sat to hear the trial case of Uncle Jesus Sainz killing his own son. Tears came out of my eyes. To me it seemed that I was at that trial hearing. I could hear voices and people around me. The feeling I got was as if the trial was being held before me. I felt anger at my great-uncle Jesus for killing his son. I wondered at the moment if Jesus felt any remorse for his son. What was he thinking as the trial went on? Great-uncle Jesus Sainz lived to be around the late 1940s before he passed away. I met Uncle Jesus in the late 1930s and early forties. He would go visit our father, Pablo, in Tempe, Arizona. I don't remember if he was still married to our Tia Carmen, who also lived in Tempe at that time. Since he was found innocent of the killing due to an old law on the books, that if a man found his wife having an affair with another man, the husband could kill both of them and be found innocent.

But in 1913, Jesus Sainz stole a horse and was given trial and found guilty and was sentenced to thirteen years in the state prison at Florence, Arizona. I do remember that when he came over to see our father, Pablo, Jesus had just been released from prison. Today is October 30, 1999, I was just remembering that it has been two and a half years that I had a six bypass heart operation. I was so sure that my heart was in a perfect condition that I would be able to finish writing the family history. I was wrong, my heart doctor named Peter Hoagland examined my heart because I was feeling tired. They found that the left side pump of my heart was not working properly, that I was heading toward a massive heart stroke. They were giving me ninety days to live. Doctor Hoagland told me of a new medical procedure that had been recently discovered.

He felt that this procedure would work for me. He told me of the dangers of the heart procedure. First, they have to stop my heart. Then they would give me an electron cardiac shock. This is to get the heart in rhythm to pump the blood throughout the body. If on the third shock the heart doesn't start, then they inject the heart with the big needle and hit the chest. If that doesn't work, they have forty-five seconds to open the chest and hand-massage the heart. I came through the procedure after the third jolt. I give thanks to our Father in Heaven and our Savior Jesus Christ for hearing all the prayers in my behalf by family members and friends. At this moment, I am feeling alert, better than I did before. Now that I am well again, I will continue our history. I will be revealing incidents that have happened in the family, in the Chavarria families, after our father and mother were married and what I have learned through my research.

In the year 1865, Great-grandfather Francisco was chief of the White Mountain Apaches. He was shot and killed at Fort Goodwin, later known as Fort Thomas. Before any white eyes (white gringos) came west to the territory of New Mexico, the White Mountain Apaches were known as the Pima Indians and Maricopas. Their hunting ground was from the Santa Cruz River where the Salt River and the Gila River come together west of Phoenix, Arizona, and all the way on both sides of the Gila River heading southeast into New Mexico at the end of the Gila River near Warm Spring heading northeast.

Including into Mexico territory, included Sonora, Mexico and Chihuahua. Both tribes, the Pimas and Maricopa Indians, were nomads. They wandered all throughout the territory that was given to them by the King of Spain as Land Grants Titles. After Mexico drove off the Spaniards to their own country, Mexico honored the Land Grants Titles of the Pimas and Maricopa Indians of present-day Arizona and New Mexico. Through records from the National Archives in Washington, I found out that this was the way our great-grandfather was able to get the 2,400 acres of land in the area of Safford and Solomonville, Arizona. That later, the United States government swindle the land away from our grandfather Francisco, son of Chief Francisco of the White Mountain Apaches. How did the U.S. government swindled the land? Very easy, they took the land into the White Mountain Apache Reservation in 1870. Then in 1872, they added the rest of his land called the San Carlos Addition into the reservation.

Then seven and a half months later in 1873, was ceded out by a presidential executive order into the public domain. Grandfather Francisco, son of Chief Francisco of the White Mountain Apaches, was living on the land that belonged to the Pima and Maricopa tribes by the Land Grants of Spain and Mexico, later under the Treaty of Guadalupe Hidalgo and the Gadsden Treaty Purchase. Our grandfather stayed on his land and became a United States citizen. Since he was living in the land already, someone must have advised him that if he didn't give his intent of keeping his land, he'll loose all of his land. He filed his intentions of keeping his land in the year 1885 under the settlers' act of 1840. Then in 1888, he signed again his declaratory statement in the Office of the Bureau of Land Management in Tucson. His first declaratory statement was filed at Florence, Arizona.

Our grandfather agreed according to the laws of the U.S. government to pay $2.25 per acre. The Act of 1840 was called the Preemption Act. This Act gave the option to commute their preemption land to a public domain homestead. When an individual converted his land to a public domain patent, the person did not have to pay for his land if he was an Indian, under the General Indian Act of 1884-87. This Act became known as the Dawes Act. This is where the silence conspiracy started to removed the land from our grandfather. The Department of the Land Office at Tucson, Arizona, gave our grandfather the wrong papers to file. Instead of giving him the Indian Application papers, they gave him the normal public domain application papers, as any white man would be given. We all know very well what an Indian looked like in the 1800s. The federal employees in the land department could very well extinguish our grandfather from any white man. They also found that he could not read or write in English.

I have found out through research of six years that grandfather's homestead application forms given to him to file were the wrong papers. Grandfather's land application should have been filed under the 1884-87 General Allotment Act, known as the Dawes Act or General Indian Act of 1887. Mr. Augene Trippel, the receiver and recorder of the General Land Office in Tucson, gave our grandfather the wrong application papers to file. This man must have been instructed what to do with Francisco's land application papers. We must remember that in 1875, this land was surveyed by the government and found that this vast area was full of gold, copper, silver, and other land treasures.

Mr. Augene Trippel made a request to change the original land certificate that came from Washington in 1895 to our grandmother Refugia Chavarria Ortiz. The final land papers state that an error was made in the homestead land certificate. That the certificate came under the names of the heir of Francisco. Yet they have not found this copy of the certificate in Washington, D.C. or in any Bureau of Land Management office in Arizona, New Mexico, or Texas. If a correction was done, where is this copy? They tell me that in the National Archives in Washington, D.C., they have been unable to find that copy. They just don't have one or someone destroyed it. I believe that we will never find that copy. Why? One may ask. Because the federal government doesn't want us to get it. It will prove that there was a silent conspiracy by the federal government in confiscating the land away from the Chavarria heirs.

It has taken nine years of in-depth research by me to be able to get all the evidence based on government and state documents to prove to the federal government that the land swindled from the Chavarrias was in earnest the U.S. government itself within their own Land Management Office in Tucson, Arizona, in 1890. This is to let the family know that today is 24 of March 2000. And of this date, the older brother Ralph and our sister Beatrice, who are still alive, still do not believe us that the land belongs to us. As of today, March 24, 2000, all the heirs of Pablo Montoya Chavarria, except four, have passed away. Ralph is 87 years of age, Beatrice is 94, Roberto Moreno Chavarria is 77 years of age, and Ramon Moreno Chavarria is 72 years of age. As of this date, the land case is in Washington, D.C. Congressman Duncan Hunter is handling the land case for me (Ramon M. Chavarria). This has not been easy getting all the documents on the land case. I have personally done all the work. I have had my share of problems not only with some government agencies, but with my own brothers Antonio, Roberto and his son Robert Jay, Antonio's stepdaughter Paula, and my sister's son Ramon Ramirez. Roberto, my own flesh and blood, wrote a nasty letter to our attorney, Mr. George Vllassis of Phoenix, Arizona, who was handling our case, that I was not in charge of the land case for the family. At the same time, his son made a phone call to Mr. Vllassis and told him that I could not be trusted.

That I was a liar and a cheat and that I was trying to keep all the money that the government might be compensating the family on the land. Then Antonio's stepdaughter and her boyfriend go over to Mr. Vllassis's office and she tells him that she is in charge, not me, her uncle. Mr. Vllassis calls me and he relates all this to me and tells me to get a signed affidavit from the rest of the family that the majority of the family is behind me. I did just that and sent George Vllassis the affidavit. Paula gets Antonio's heirs plus Ramon, our sister Josephina's oldest son, to join her in removing me out as the person in charge of the case. After this episode, Mr. George Vllassis wrote me his resignation. He stated that he could not work with the family on this land case. It seemed to him that all in the family wanted their hands on the case and he could not do the job required of him.

I called him and thanked him for all the trouble he tried to iron out with the family and told him that I understood him. I said, "George, if I was in your shoes, I would do the same thing you're doing in resigning." Then I asked him for some advice of what to do in getting another lawyer. These are his exact words to me, "Ray, let your brother and his son, Jay, handle it. This is what they really want to do. They see that you have done all the heavy work. Know they want the glory that will go with winning the case. They will get themselves a lawyer after they try to convince you that both of them can fight Paula and her family in the land case because of Jay's experience as a probate lawyer." He says, "Let them have it. I guarantee that within a month. They will be calling you for help."

Mr. Vllassis was right on the money. They called me if they could handle the land case for the family. I turned it over to them. Within a few days, they wanted an affidavit giving them my authorization to find a lawyer and take the case over to themselves. I gave them the signed affidavit and they did get a lawyer by the name of April O'Brien from Las Vegas, Nevada. After they hired the lawyer, Roberto calls me to ask for help. Miss April O'Brien, the lawyer, wanted to see if I could get the congressman (Duncan Hunter) to work with her office in getting the case before Congress. I had to think very hard on this decision of getting the congressman involved with my brother and his son in helping them on the land case. I had a long discussion with Mr. Catalino "Cato" Cedillo, the chief executive officer for Congressman Duncan Hunter's El Cajon, California, Congressional Office.

The Congressional Office has been helping me with this land case since March 1994, after my brother Tony sent the homestead certificate to me so that I could see it. This is the time that the congressman and Mr. Cato Cedillo viewed the land document. Congressman Hunter offered to help me with this land case. They have been helping me along, since 1994. Mr. Cedillo advised me that the Congressional Office would continue to work with me and not my brother (Roberto) or his son Robert Jay.

They told me that if I wanted the lawyers involved with me, they had no problem with that. The congressman told me, "Ray, I don't know your brother or his son. I offered to help you on this as a friend. You helped me get elected to Congress in the beginning. Now it's my turn to help you on this land matter. My office will continue to work with you until this land case is solved one way or the other." I told Mr. Cato Cedillo that only the lawyers would be calling him on the land case. But I was wrong. My brother Roberto and his son started to call from their home in Las Vegas, Nevada, to the Congressional Office. They got Mr. Cedillo very upset that he called me and told me what my brother and his son were doing. I called Roberto and told him that those calls were hurting our support of the Congressional Office of the congressman.

What they did after my call is that they went and talked with April O'Brien, their lawyer, and had a letter of instruction sent to Mr. Cato Cedillo not to deal with any of the Chavarria families on this matter of the land. Little do they know that I am the one that is running the show. Every time that they call the office or their lawyers, I am informed of the conversation of what took place. When the lawyers sent the land summary to the Congressional Office in November 1999, I was called to the office to view the summary before the office send it to the Washington office for review before sending it to the Judiciary Legislative Committee for a special bill for the Chavarria families. Mr. Cedillo asked me to take it home and review it and make any changes that I felt needed.

During the Christmas holidays, I studied the summary and found it to contain many mistakes in spelling and date of events and not a strong summary. I made the corrections and provided a supplement and a larger brief with all the information and documents that I had in my possession. A large number of documents and letters that my brother and his son don't have in their possession went in those briefs. I kept many of the land documents from my brother and his son because I don't trust them after what they have done to me. To this day, April 14, 2000, Robert Jay owes me over eighteen thousand dollars and his father, six hundred dollars. Robert Jay hasn't spoken to me in over three years. This is because he did the same thing to other members of the family. None of the family knew that he was doing this to get money from each one of us. So how can I trust him on this land case in case we win? He might want to keep all of the money to himself and his father and leave the family in the dark. I have taken steps to safeguard the family's interest of each heir. This will be done by the Congressional Office and the lawyers and myself with the congressman. This case is already in the hands of those that will be deciding what course to take for its success.

I have in my possession microfilms (six rolls) from the archives concerning my ancestors and government documents of the Indian Wars of the Indians since 1790 to 1886. I have found that our great-grandfather Francisco, chief of the White Mountain Coyoteros, was involved in many Indian raids into Mexico. I will be giving a history of our Indian heritage. This I am doing so that my own family can be proud of their Indian ancestors.

In the year 1790, Apacheria was in the Arizona territory. It was not known yet as part of Arizona. Mexico was the owner of California, Arizona, New Mexico, Texas. Part of Arizona was in the state of Chihuahua and the western part was in the state of Sonora. The State of Chihuahua covered what is known as the state of New Mexico.

The Chavarria history, as far as records indicate, started in this two areas of Mexico in 1790. First, let me give a small part of our Indian ancestors. The Apaches were a warlike and nomadic people who roamed the Southwest, preferring to live in rugged, inaccessible mountains and equally at home in the march desert. The word Apache had two meanings. *E-patch*, loosely interpret to mean "man," taken from the Yuman Indian. The second meaning comes from the Zuni word *apachu*, which means "enemy." The Apaches called themselves *tinneh, tinde,* or *inde,* which translates to "man" or "people." The Chiricahuas consisted of four bands. The eastern Chiricahuas were known as the Mimbres, Copper mines, Warm Springs, Mogollon, and all-encompassing Gilas, names describing geographic locations where they lived. Their territory was west of the Rio Grande in New Mexico, and lived in the Cuchillo, Black, Mimbres, Moggollon, Pinos Altos, Victoria, and Florida mountain ranges.

Their leaders from the 1820s to 1870s were Mano Mucha, Fuerte, Cuchillo Negro, Itan, Mangas Coloradas, Delgadito, Victorio, Nana, and Loco. To the Apaches, they were the Chihennes, or red-painted people.

The second band, called the Southern Chiricahuas, were known to Mexicans and Americans as the Janeros, Carrizalenos, and Pinery Apaches. They inhabited the mountains along the U.S.-Mexican border served as their homeland. They also roamed deep into the vast Sierra Madre in the Mexican states of Chihuahua and Sonora. Occasionally, they wandered across the border into present-day southeastern Arizona and southwestern New Mexico. The Janeros Indian people were so named for their friendly relations at Janos, a small town in northern Chihuahua. Their leaders from 1820s to the 1870s were Juan Diego Compa, Juan Jose Compa, followed by Coleto Amarillio, Arviso, Laceris, Galindo, Natiza, and Juh. The Carrizalenos lived south of the Janeros people near Carrizal, Chihuahua. Their most prominent leaders in the 1820s and 1830s were Jasquedega and Cristobal. In the 1840s, Francisquillo, Francisco, this is our great-grandfather, and Cigattito assumed leadership, followed by Cojinillin and Felipe in the 1850s. Both groups were hit hard by Mexican campaigns from 1830s to the early 1860s. This is the time that our great-grandfather came to live in the Gila River Valley of the White Mountains and Graham Mountain area.

The third Band of Chokonens, the one that Cochise was a member, was the Central Chiricahuas. Their homeland was Southeastern Arizona, particularly the Dragoons Mountain, Dos Cabezas Mountains, and the Chiricahua Mountains.

They also ranged north to the Gila River, east into southwestern New Mexico, and south into the Sierra Madre. The mountains along the U.S.-Mexico border gave them sanctuary from the Mexican and American troops. From 1820s to 1870s, their leaders were Pisago Cabezon, Relles, Matias, Tapita, Yrigollen, Miguel, Narbona, Carro, Posito Moraga, Esquinaline, and Cochise. In all the history books written, this band of Indians were called the Chiricahua Indians. Prior to the white man given them different names according to the areas that they lived, they were known as the Chokonens.

The fourth group of Indians were the Bedonkohes during historical times. They became part of Cochise's band. The famous Geronimo was born into this band of Bedonkohes Indians.

Our great-grandfather Francisco was given the Indian name Fresco. He became a very close associate of Cochise. They both planned raids into Mexico to settlements as Fronterra, Arispe, Chinapa, Nacozari, Bavispe, Bacoachi, Cuchuta, Janos, Ascecion, Corralitos, Carrizal, and Galeana. The name of great-grandfather was given to him because he was born at the mouth of the Gila River and there was a small river called Fresco River in the territory of New Mexico that connected to the Gila River. At this time, 1843, this part was still in the Mexican territory of Chihuahua, The band of Indians his family belong to were the Chokonens (Chiricahuas). Mangas Coloradas was the leader of this band.

Great-grandfather was a chief in the early 1850s. He allied with Cochise to make raids into Sonora very often. What my father told me about him, my grandmother Refugia told my father some of his history. She is also the one that told my father about his father who was the son of Chief Francisco. My grandfather was trained as a warrior by his father. He also rode with him in raids into Mexico. What I have been able to find about him in books is that he was a well-built man. They describe him as being five feet ten and a half inches height and weigh about 185 pound and solid muscle, and a handsome face. Although I have tried to find more history on our great-grandfather, I have only the information that the National Archives have been able to lead me to in the microfilm they have of the 1850-60s. The rest of the information has come through books that were written by those cavalry soldiers that served during the Indian Wars of the 1860s to the 1886. Indian historians have advised me to read these books for more information on the Echeveriah families, especially *On the Border with Crook* by John G. Bourke. This book has lot of history of the Valley of the San Pedro where my mother Rita Soto Moreno was born at old Camp Grant, later Fort Breckenridge, near the mouth of the Ariviapa River flowing into the San Pedro River.

This vast area of the Gila River and Salt River west of what is Phoenix, Arizona, now all the way to Ojo Caliente at the end of the Gila River in New Mexico to the Mexican border into Mexico was our great-grandfather's stumping grounds. Our grandfather Francisco Chavarria was born at Warm Springs in 1843, but he grew up in Janos Chihuahua, Mexico. Francisco (El Fresco), our great-grandfather went on his raids into the surrounding towns of Sonora, Mexico. When the Mexican troops would follow them, they would head into the United States into the mountains of the Gila, Dos Cabezas, Mogollon, Burro, and the Chiricahua Mountains. In some cases, the U.S. Cavalry would chase them into the Mexican side of the border.

The other book to read is *Cochise Chiricahua Apache Chief* by Edwin R. Sweeney. This book has plenty of history on our great-grandfather. When our father, Pablo, told me that his grandfather was shot and killed at Camp Goodwin by the U.S. Cavalry in 1865, I honestly believed that he was making this up. As I started to do my in-depth search on the family, the National Archives in Washington, D.C. sent me this roll of microfilm where I could locate our great-grandfather Francisco (El Fresco), White Mountain Apache chief. I found out that what our father had told me concerning his grandfather was true. I have in my possession the microfilm concerning his death.

This is what was written about his death at Fort Goodwin in this book. This is an account of his death in 1865. First, on November 10, troops at Fort Goodwin gunned down Eastern White Mountain leader Francisco allegedly while trying to escape. Francisco had been imprisoned for his part in the Cienega attack the previous summer.

Moreover, a falling out of sorts had come between Cochise's Chokonens and the White Mountain and Pinal bands of the western Apaches. Both were said to be "bitter against the Cochise's band of Indians who were undoubtedly the perpetrators of all the emigrant road massacres" in the past few years. This is what was written in this book *Cochise: Chiricahua Apache Chief.* In the microfilm in my possession, the *Tucson Citizen* newspaper wrote an editorial in 1865 and this is what it they wrote.

DEATH OF AN APACHE CHIEF

Col. Robert Pollock at Fort Goodwin, informs General Mason, under date of November 11th, of the killing of an Apache Chief of the White Mountain tribe known as "Francisco the butcher," and who has been notorious for many years in the robberies; and murders-committed; by his tribe, Francisco was arrested by Capt. Kennedy for complicity in the massacre of a German family, and others from Texas, on the Cienega, twenty-eight miles from Tucson, on the Apache Pass road a short time since as well as to induce the tribe to give up three children captured at the same massacre and who are yet in the Indian's hands. Col. Pollock says; "On the night of the 10th in about 10 o'clock, the prisoner applied to the acting sergeant of the guard, Wm. O. Pascoe. Corporal, Uo. 1, 1st. Cav. C.V., for permission to go to the rear, which was granted, and he was companied by a Corporal and two men.

On arriving at a point about ninety yards from the guard house, the prisoner, (who was a large and splendidly proportioned man) started and sprang off, when the guard fired several shots at him, nearly all of which took effect, and he fell, dying instantly, shot through the brain, heart and abdomen.; I found that the rivets of the shackles in the left leg and hand had been filed off and taken out completely liberating the prisoner. Francisco's death has made little or no impression on the Indians in the vicinity, They visit the post daily, and appear to be satisfied that death is the inevitable result of attempts to escape from the guard house, besides, the deceased was much feared among them and it seems that many breathe easier now that they have no more to fear from him.

The wording is the same way the article appeared on the *Tucson Centennial* in 1865. These reporters wanted to get the citizens of the territory hating Indians and also to sell newspapers. The white men never understood that the Indian was not a savage. They were peaceful family clusters respecting each other's land. They lived apart from each other and when a male married a maiden from another tribe, he would have to move into the girl's family and become a member of that family's tribe. History reveals that it was the white man that introduced the savage part of mutilation and scalping was taught by them to the Mexicans. The Mexican government started to pay $250 per Indian scalps in the early 1846. Mexico hired James Kirker to kill Apaches and they would pay him a bounty of $250 per scalp.

This man named James Kirker was a very evil man. If he and his men couldn't find Indians, he would kill Mexicans and scalp them, and bring the scalps as bounty. There was no difference in the Indian black hair and the Mexican black hair. Since the Mexican is a descended of Indian blood, James Kirker got away with it for a while. The Mexican government finally got wise to what he was doing and fired him from their services.

The southwest Indians still remember the James Kirker Massacre at Galeana, Mexico. This man and his party of cutthroat butchers ambushed this Indian Rancheria and killed all who lived there. They killed all the Indians while they were sleeping early in the morning.

PRESS RELEASE

Never in their life would Tony, Ramon, Bob, and Bob's son Jay Chavarria would ever dream that they would uncover one of Arizona's most bizarre land fraud in its history. Little did they realized that a historical document that was never known to the Chavarria Families would come out of it's hidden place and show up one hundred years later, and change the life of each one of the brothers and nephew. What is so bizarre is that at no time in its history did the Chavarria's, including the legal owner of the document, Pablo Montoya Chavarria, ever saw or heard of such a historical legal document.

Pablo M. Chavarria would have been one of Arizona's richest land barons in the turn of the century (1896). Prior to this history of the Chavarria's, let's go back to the year 1824, when Pablo Chavarria was not born yet, including his only sister Carmen and his older brother Francisco Jr. Intensive research that has required the brothers and nephew to utilize all of their education, special job skills, knowledge, and abilities in order that an in-depth investigation was properly conducted. That as their research lead them into the family past history, and would reveal how this land, twenty four hundred acres of prime agricultural land, including the riches minerals that can be found and water rights, was swindled out of the Chavarrias, Francisco Chavarria Sr.'s heirs.

With the help of one California Congressman, Congressman Duncan Hunter (R) from San Diego, California. He was very instrumental in helping the family obtain certain land documents from the Safford, Arizona County Court House. The documents showed that Francisco Chavarria was the legal owner of this property. The Congressman also was instrumental in setting a special meeting with the Senator of Arizona John McCain. Senator McCain is a member of the Office of Indian Affairs in Washington, D.C. The office staff of the Senator in Phoenix, Arizona, were very helpful in helping the family in obtaining information and documents from the Nation Archives in Washington and Suitland, Maryland, that actual revealed how grandfather had come in possession of this land.

As historical documents started to come to the family from State and Federal Offices and the Laguna Niguel, Fort Worth, and Tucson. Not only did the brothers and nephew found that some of the Documents were fraudulent, but that the signatures of their father and uncle were also fraudulent. They had this historical documents examined by a retired Federal Bureau of Investigation hand writing expert who worked as a federal employee out of the office of Documents and Forgery. This man has his own business in Chula Vista, California. He examined the documents and found the names of Francisco and Pablo are fraudulent signatures.

Through the office of Senator John McCain, member of the Indian Affairs Committee, the Bureau of Indian Affair of the Department of the Interior, Washington, D.C. came the information of how Grandfather Francisco Chavarria received the land. In 1824, Great-grandfather lived on the land, that belonged to the territory of Mexico, known at that time as Chihuahua, Mexico. This land that ran from the Southeast to up North, then Southwest to the Pacific Ocean, covered California, Utah, Nevada, Arizona, Colorado, New Mexico, and Texas, belonged to Mexico, before the Treaty of Guadalupe Hidalgo of 1848. After the Treaty of Guadalupe Hidalgo was signed in February 2, 1848, Mexico agreed to sell to the United States of America.

The Treaty in article VIII stipulates Mexicans now established in territories previously belonging to Mexico, and which remain for the future within the limits of the United States, as defined by the present treaty, shall be free to continue where they reside, or to remove at any time to the Mexican Republic, retaining the property, which they posses in the said territory or disposing thereof and removing the proceeds wherever they please, without their being subjected, on this account, to any contribution, tax, or charge whatever.

Those who shall prefer to remain in the said territories, may either retain the title and rights of Mexican Citizens, or acquire those of Citizens of the United States. But they shall be under the obligation to make their selection within one year from the date of exchange of ratifications of this treaty and those who shall remain in the said territories after the expiration of that year, without having declared their intention to retain the character of Mexicans, shall be considered to have elected to become Citizens of the United States. Great-grandfather remained in his land as an American Citizen. In the year 1843, his wife gave birth to his first son, named Francisco. In 1852, (our grandfather) his second son is born naming him Trinidad. Then in 1855, his third son is born named Regino. The United States acquired the southern territory, to the Mexican Border through the Gadsden Treaty Purchase of December 30, 1853. The United States paid Mexico the sum of $10,000,000 for additional lands below the Gila River, taking the land of Francisco Chavarria (Solomonville) away from him, granted to him by Spain, honored by Mexico until the land sale to the United States of America.

The land was incorporated in the territory of New Mexico by the Act of August 4, 1854, and the Arizona Territory was created from that part of the New Mexico Territory which lay West of the Southwest corner of the Colorado Territory by the Act of February 24, 1863. This land was known as Tierra Apacheria (Apache Land) by the Mexican Government of the Republic of Mexico. After the Gadsden Treaty Purchase of 1853, it became known as the Arizona Territory, then in 1912, it became the State of Arizona.

All this years the Chavarria family is still cultivating the land and producing agricultural goods. Then on January 31, 1870, Major Henry M. Robert recommended that the War Department set apart the White Mountain Indian Reservation in the Arizona Territory. The White Mountain Indian Reservation was formally established by U.S. President Grant by executive order dated November 9, 1871. A second Executive Order by President Grant dated December 14, 1872, added the San Carlos Division—later known as the San Carlos Indian Reservation to the White Mountain Indian Reservation. The San Carlos Indian Reservation straddled the Valley of the upper Gila River, with its South boundary being "a line 15 miles south of the parallel to the Gila River." (Please note that at this time Francisco and his wife are still living on their land inside the San Carlos Indian Reservation.)

The Treaty of Peace, Friendship, Limits, and Settlement with the Republic of Mexico, better known as the treaty of Guadalupe Hidalgo, gave Francisco Chavarria the protection of his property. Article IX states, Mexicans who in the territories aforesaid, shall not preserve the character of the Citizens of the Mexican Republic, conformable with what is stipulated in the proceeding article, shall be incorporated into the Union of the United States and be admitted at the proper time (to be judged of by the Congress of the United States) to the enjoyment of all the rights of Citizens of the United States, according to the principles of the Constitution; and in the mean time shall be maintained and protected in the free enjoyment of their Liberty and property, and secured in the free exercise of their religion without restriction. The land granted to the Grandfather of the Chavarria families, thus came to be within the San Carlos Indian Reservation as of December 14, 1872. Due to petitions and political pressures by residents of the Arizona Territory, six and ½ months later, a third Executive Order was issued out by President Grant dated the 5th of August 1873, under the recommendation of Acting Secretary, B.R. Cowen, of the Department of the Interior Washington, D.C. July 30, 1873, the letter states:

> Respectfully submitted to the President with the recommendation that all that portion of the valley of the Gila River in the territory of Arizona hitherto included in the San Carlos Division of the White Mountain Indian Reservation as established by Executive order dated December 14, 1872, lying East of and above the site of old Camp Goodwin, be restored to the Public Domain, as recommended by the Acting Commissioner of Indian Affairs.

The response came from the Executive Mansion, August 5, 1873.

> Agreeable to the above recommendation of the Acting Secretary of the Interior, it is hereby ordered that the land therein described be restored to the Public domain, Signed U.S. Grant.

Yet at this time, the family of Francisco is still living on their land; their Great-grandfather left the land to his three sons, as his heirs. The youngest son became an alcoholic and started selling part of the land that belonged to the three brothers, to maintain his drinking habit.

One may wonder and say, how could he sell the land when it had gone into public domain? The Chavarria brothers and nephew believe the silent conspiracy started with the above Executive order of July 30, 1873, to make Francisco's land into public domain land and take its minerals out of the land, all of its precious metals. Somebody had to give the orders on this conspiracy; a high Government official had to be the one. Who developed the conspiracy?

The Chavarrias have that proof where this conspiracy started and by whom. Through historical documents and family history, passed from father to son and Government historical documents, the family has discovered that Francisco, in his youth, rode with Cochise, Chief of the Chiricahua Indians, as a young warrior. Cochise send Francisco with his warriors after some of Geronimo's warrior's who escaped from the San Carlos Reservation.

The chase took them to the Salt River Crossing in Tempe, Arizona. It was called Hayden Ferry Crossing at that time. The reason for Francisco to ride with Cochise warriors was that he was also acquainted with Geronimo. Geronimo and his warriors on certain occasions, he would camp overnight on grandfather's land close to the Gila River on their way to scout white settlements or raids into Mexico. His mission was to try to persuade Geronimo's warriors to give themselves up to the U.S. Army Cavalry.

Cochise warriors did not find Geronimo or any of his warriors. This fact of history, was told by Pablo Montoya Chavarria, father to Ramon (Ray) Moreno Chavarria when he was twelve years of age. Pablo also told his son Ramon that his father left his name carved with his knife at the old Casa Vieja inside of one of the adobe walls. The warriors stayed overnight and slept at the old Casa Viega and left early in the morning back to San Carlos.

Ramon saw his grandfather's name on that wall when he was twelve years of age. The name of Francisco is still carved on that wall after all this years. The adobe walls are plastered, and it has preserved the name because they plastered over the name. The place is famous now for its steak dinners in Tempe, Arizona. Also that he had a freight wagon train of twenty wagons driven by axons, hauling ore minerals from Bisbee, Arizona, to the gold smelters in Morenci, Clifton, Miami, and Superior, all in Arizona. There were times that his wagon train would stop for a few days to rest the axons and his wagon crew in Tombstone, Arizona.

The oldest brother told Ramon a year before he passed away to a better world that Grandfather Francisco knew the Earp brothers, Wyatt, Virgil, and Morgan. We can only take his word for it because the Earp brothers were in Tombstone, Arizona (the town too tough to die), in those late years of the 1860 as law enforcement Marshals of the Arizona Territory and Francisco did pass through Tombstone on his way to Solomonville where he lived and had his land. Before he started his business of hauling freight, he rounded wild horses and broke them in, and sold them to the U.S. Army Cavalry. In the Month of August 1973, our father Pablo M. Chavarria is hospitalized with a broken hip. Ramon spends two weeks visiting his father every day. Ramon lives in San Diego, California. He was employed by the United States Navy as a civil Servant, with the position of Equal Employment Opportunity, Affirmative Action Officer.

His father tells him for the first time. Tells his son Ramon (Ray) that the man he knew as his grandfather (Blas Ortiz) is not his grandfather. Pablo then reveals to his son the truth about his father Francisco Chavarria. He tells Ramon that his father (Francisco) died in a freak horse accident, chasing three renegade Indians who had been following his wagon train for days. He said that grandfather's horse stumbled on a rock and that grandfather flew over his horses' neck and hit a big boulder head on, and died on the spot.

That all of the land that belong to him and his brother, went to his fathers brother Regino, because they were co-partners on the land, and that his uncle sold all of the land they had lived on and worked the farm. That one cold morning four vaqueros (four cowboys) with guns and rifles came to the ranch, showed their mother Refugia (grandmother) some papers and that their mother told them that they had to leave the ranch because their uncle Regino had sold the ranch and they had to move else where.

Pablo told his son Ramon that his mother (grandmother) married a year after the death of our grandfather. That his mother married a farmhand that worked for her. Our father Pablo was seven years of age and he grew to love this man as his father. Then he tells his son Ramon, "Your grandfather and grandmother were Apache Indians and your mother was also Apache Indian like I am." Ramon takes notes because he is doing Genealogy to trace the family history and to write a book on the Chavarria family tree.

Ramon never again talked to his father again. Ramon had to return to San Diego. His father remained in the hospital and died a week after that. Ramon mentioned all this to his brother Antonio (Tony) what their father had revealed to him about being Apache Indians. This is in 1973, and is left at that, except that Tony started to help the Indians in High School as an Indian Counselor to the present time. Then in 1994, Tony calls Ramon, his brother, to tell him what he found in our old house in Tempe, Arizona.

He tells his brother that due to his heart operation, he had forgotten to look at the contents that he brought from our old house that he had stored away in his garage. This is how the lives of the three brothers and nephew came to find out what this historical document did to change their lives. On August 1990, Tony was invited by Mrs. Rose Montanez, our stepbrother's ex-wife from our father's third marriage (Gilbert V. Montanez). Gilbert bought the old house from our father Pablo and let him live there and his mother rent free. Rose's invitation was to see if Tony wanted any of our fathers and mother's pictures for keepsake for remembrance. Tony was more interested in finding fathers favorite belt buckle that had a violin engraved on it.

The belt buckle was an award from the old work program that was called WPA (the Workman Program Act). Paula, Tony's daughter, saw a metal box hidden on one of the walls of the house and Tony recognized the metal box. This box is where our father kept all of his important papers. Paula carried it to her father's truck. This Metal fishing tackle box used to belong to Blas Ortiz. Blas is the individual that married our grandmother Refugia in 1892 after the death of our grandfather Francisco.

After the death of Blas Ortiz, our father Pablo kept that metal box as a memento. Blas always carried a leather pouch around his waist and no one ever touched it. He never let go of it. This is the metal box that our brother Tony and his daughter Paula found the historical document and other fraudulent documents that led to the discovery of the silent conspiracy to swindle the land from the Chavarria's Heirs.

The Chavarria Family has turned all of the documents to Congressman Duncan Hunter and their lawyers, who will represent them in Federal System Court. In this swindle, there are members of The Church of Jesus Christ of Later Day Saints, who were sent by the Church to settle and start the work of the Lord amongst the Indians (Lamanites) in the Arizona Territory, who squatted the land, then left it and another would come and do the same thing. At the present time, a member of the Mormon faith lives on that land.

After the Chavarrias and investigators have gone through all this documents, they have all come to one solid conclusion. They know what Agency in the federal government was involved on the swindle of the land and State Officials, such as a Notary Public, Lawyers, two Federal Judges, a court clerk, and a Federal employee of the Bureau of Land Management, known today as the Department of the Interior.

One must remember that the land of the Chavarrias was protected by the Treaty of Guadalupe Hidalgo and the Gadsden Treaty Purchase of the rights of protection to all United States Citizens under the U.S. Constitution, of illegal seizure of private property under due process of law, according to our Constitution. The Chavarrias believe that all the land and mineral, water, agricultural rights should be restored to the family. The Chavarria family has in their possession a Federal Homestead trust patent. The certificate is signed by the President of the United States of America, Grover Cleveland, April 15, 1896. The land is 136 and 94/100 of an acre. It's located in Solomon, Arizona at the close range of the Gila River. The certificate was filed on the 9th of May by Augene Trippel (county register), at Tucson, Arizona land office. The deed is recorded on the 26 of May 1896 at the request of Blas Ortiz. Mr. Manuel Leon was the county recorder. The Chavarrias Tony, Ramon, Roberto, and Jay (Robert Jr.) wonder why their grandfather had to file for a homestead land claim when the land was his already in the first place. Francisco Chavarria Sr. left this land to his two sons Francisco Jr. and Pablo Montoya Chavarria. We are the sons and daughters of Pablo M. Chavarria, the last survivor (son), whom he left the land as an inheritance to stay in the family forever. We are Pablo Montoya Chavarria's heirs. We are full-blooded Apache Indians.

Researched and written and typed by
Ramon (Ray) Moreno Chavarria

After finishing the first part of the family history, I have taken some time to do other things that I had to finish. I committed myself to helping Miss Betsey Bayless, who is the secretary of state of Arizona at that time. She is campaigning to see if she can become the next governor of Arizona. Your mother accompanied me to Arizona last year on October 10, 2001. We attended a fiesta that was planned by the Tempe Historical Museum.

The sole purpose of this fiesta is to bring the residents of the surrounding areas to know the history of the Hispanic and Native Americans who have contribute so much to the history of Tempe since 1870. My job was to show Miss Bayless the museum and to introduce her to the public at large. The Tempe Fiesta was a very successful event that day. There were over thirty-five thousand people who attended the fiesta. My brother Ralph A. Chavarria and his band played for the fiesta function. Ralph, who is known as Chapito Chavarria, has played all over Arizona and California in his younger years.

Ralph's band still packs them in (the people, that is). The wife and I met a lot of our friends there attending the fiesta; friends that went to school with us and continued our friendship with each other. They had food stands all over the place and the food was very good. They had different dance groups to perform on stage. They were very good dancers. The secretary of state really enjoyed her visit to Tempe that day and I was very happy that I was able to help her get some commitments from people that gave their word that they were going to vote for her this coming election. I do hope that they do. Miss Bayless is a very smart woman. Arizona can benefit from her talents and what is needed for the people as a whole in that state. Prior to going to Tempe on that trip, I had been in communication with the Bureau of Land Management in Phoenix concerning the Chavarria land case.

I had been having phone conversations with two of their land law examiners by the names of Mrs. Ivy Garcia and Alyson Johnson. Mrs. Garcia is the person in charge of the Land Law Examiners in the Bureau of Land Management. This bureau comes under the United States Department of the Interior. They have all the land briefs that I compiled since 1994. These are briefs that have all the letters that I have written to different department of government agencies and State agencies in Arizona, New Mexico, Washington, D.C., Texas, California, and Mexico. This briefs have all the documents that I have been able to obtain from these agencies to prove the Chavarria land case that the United States government failed to issue our grandfather Francisco Chavarria an Indian trust patent, under the guardianship of the United States of America under the General Allotment Act of 1884, known as the General Indian Allotment Act or Dawes Act of 1884.

During this time of October, the Bureau of Land Management in Phoenix, Arizona, had been planning to meet me in Arizona. The purpose of this meeting was that the Department of the Interior from Washington, D.C. was sending their top land law examiner by the name of Richard Fairchild to meet with all of us. That is Mrs. Garcia, Mrs. Johnson, and two individuals of the Department of Indian Affairs. We were to meet on

October 14, 2001, at the Phoenix office. That meeting didn't take place. The persons that were to come from Washington, D.C. could not make it over because of another land case they were involved with. This is the case of Mrs. Elouise Cobell of Wyoming. This case is bigger than the Chavarria land case. It involves about five hundred thousand Native Americans who have been cheated out of their land trust funds. While I was in Arizona helping the secretary of state (Betsey Bayless) in her campaign, I made a phone call to the Bureau of Land Management to see if they had planned another meeting with me. Their answer was no. They said it would be about ninety days before we could plan to meet. I mentioned this to the secretary of state to see if she could help me. I called Mr. Cedillo from the office of Congressman Hunter in El Cajon, California. I mentioned to him that I couldn't get the meeting with the law examiners in Phoenix while I was there campaigning for the secretary of state of Arizona.

I told him that I had talked to the secretary about my problem in getting the meeting set in order to present the Chavarria land case and the new evidence of documents that I had found. Mr. Cedillo asked, "What can I do to help you?" I said, "Why don't you call the secretary of state of Arizona and see if she can help your office in getting an appointment to meet with those people of the Department of the Interior in Phoenix, Arizona?" Mr. Cedillo said to me, "I'll call her as soon as you and I get off the phone." I got back to California on the twenty-first of October. Two days later, Mr. Cedillo called to tell me that the secretary of state of Arizona had arranged a meeting for us to meet with the law examiners from Washington, D.C. in Phoenix, Arizona. We flew to Phoenix and met with the law examiners. I presented the Chavarria land case to them. While I was presenting the land case, one attorney asked me, "Mr. Chavarria, is the family claiming the land under the Treaty of Guadalupe Hidalgo or the Gadsden Treaty Purchase?" He then stated, "If you are, then you have no case. The Supreme Court of the United States passed a law that any lands granted to individuals under Spanish, French, or Mexican land grants were not valid anymore whatsoever." I stood up and said, "Ladies and gentlemen, the Chavarrias are claiming their land under this document signed by the president of the United States of America in 1896. This is a federal document that states that the United States government recognizes Francisco Chavarria as a citizen of the United States of America entitled to a federal homestead land grant."

"This is the document that we, as heirs of Francisco Chavarria, are claiming land compensation, land benefits, and punitive damages for over one hundred and twelve years." This is when they took time to talk things over. After they came back to the meeting room, Mrs. Ivy Garcia said, "After reviewing the new documentation, we find that the Chavarrias do have a claim. We find that the Chavarrias can request a correction on their grandfather's homestead certificate by filling these documents now and the filing fee of one hundred ($100) dollars to cover the correction examination of all the documents that the Chavarria family has introduced to the Department of the Interior." Today is March 9, 2002. The Department of Land Management in Arizona has not come to a decision yet on our case. It has been almost ninety days that I submitted the forms for a correction on our grandfather's homestead certificate. I am waiting to see what their decision will be. I honestly believe that with all the documentation that I have submitted, they can only go one way and that is to correct the homestead certificate to be an Indian trust patent under the guardianship of the United States government.

During all this time that I have been doing all this research, writing letters, and making phone calls to the Bureau of Land management in Arizona, I had an encounter, a hostile and usually brief confrontation, with my brother Roberto and his son Robert Jay concerning their lawyers. It seems that they want me to stop what I am doing on the land case and give them all my information—documents and briefs—that I developed to send to the Bureau of the Interior in Phoenix, Arizona. They also want me off our land case completely. They want the case in order that if the Department of the Interior goes in our favor and the United States government makes a settlement with the Chavarria family, they want to handle all the money and give the Chavarria heirs what they want to give. I do not agree with what they want to do. I wrote them a letter, telling them that I will not get off the case and I will not turn my work over to them whatsoever.

They must be thinking that I am that dumb to believe that I will just drop off our family land case like that. I am going to stay on this case until it is finished, one way or the other. I have received letters of protest from the heirs that have an interest on this case. They do not want Roberto or his son Robert Jay to handle the case for the heirs. They want me to continue on the land case. Last week, I wrote a letter to the attorneys that my brother hired to handle the land case for the Chavarrias. In this letter, I advised them that my brother or his son are not authorized to represent the Chavarrias in any land case. That in order to do so, they have to have the Chavarria heirs sign an authorization agreement with their attorneys that they have signed a contract. This is the only way that they can represent the Chavarria heirs. This would make it confusing for the attorneys because they have already signed an agreement with me to represent them on this land case and Congressman Duncan Hunter (R).

Today is March 18, 2002. I have not yet received an answer from the Department of Land Management of Phoenix, Arizona. Their decision is to search all the documents that I have submitted as proof that the homestead certificate was indeed an Indian trust patent under the guardianship of our government. That it was the United States Government that took it out of trust in 1890. Friday, March 22, 2002, I made a call to the Bureau of Land Management in Phoenix, Arizona, to find out the status of the Chavarria land case. Mrs. Alyson Johnson was the person that answered the phone. Mrs. Johnson related to me that the department was still looking at the files. She advised me that they would come to a decision on the case in the middle of April. She said that they are checking all the documents that I submitted as proof.

JULY 29, 1995

STEVE TITLA
GENERAL COUNSEL
SAN CARLOS APACHE TRIBE
P.O. BOX 701
GLOBE, ARIZONA 85502

Dear Steve:

Although I have not received a final reply in response to my inquiries, I wanted to assure you that I am doing everything I can, and will continue my efforts until we have finalized the Chavarria's case. However, we have uncovered some very valuable concrete information!

We have discovered that the property that is in question has had seven mining companies, in the year of July 31, 1899, removed more than $22,000,000.00 of gold ore from said property.

a)   Great Western Copper, Gold and Silver mining and reduction company.
b)   The Copper Bell mining chain.
c)   The Stanley Peach mining company.
d)   The Copper Giant mining chain.
e)   The Big Bug mining chain.
f)   Treasure Box mining company.
g)   Columbia mining chain.

All monies was assigned for deposit through the Consolidated National Bank of Tucson, Arizona.

Please be assured of my continuing interest in this matter. I will be in touch with you again as soon as I have something further to report.

Sincerely,

John McCain
United States Senator

JM/xka
Enclosure

Acknowledgments

The author wish to acknowledge the following persons for their contribution in the development of this Family book history. To my dear and loving wife Margarita Chavarria, who came up with the original idea of me writing the family roots for our grandchildren. Father John Ancharski, Priest of the Lady of Guadalupe Catholic Church in Solomon, Arizona, for family church records, Paul Amado Chavarria, Deceased brother, who related early family history. And a special thanks to my good friend and neighbor, Evelia Delayo for helping me have faith in my self to finish the last fifty pages of the book.

Biography

Ray Chavarria was born in a small western town, by the name of Tempe, Arizona. He attended his education at a School named Tempe Grammar School. Ray graduated from Jr High and was a school drop out. He worked the agricultural fields in his youth. Married in 1945 to Margarita H. Perea whom he met in his last year of school. Enlisted in the service of our Country during the end of the War in 1945 in the United States Air Force, Took gunnery school on the B-29 aircraft, The closing of the Gunnery School Ray chose Cook and Baker School. Was assigned to the 8th Air Force Base in Roswell, New Mexico under Col. Robert Tibbet who pilot the B-29, that drop the Atomic Bomb in Hiroshima, Japan. Ray was assign as one of his personal cooks. Upon his discharge, Ray enlisted in the Air Force standby reserve for twenty years, was a member of the Arizona Air National Guard for five (5) years.

Ray Chavarria has served his Country well. He went to work for the United States Government as a civilian employee. Worked his way from General helper to Painter, than Aircraft Painter at the Naval Air Station, North Island, California, San Diego, California. Ray continued his education under certain programs for navy and civilian employees to get their High School education and College diplomas. Ray received his College Diploma in Business Administration and Political Science in 1980. In his position as an Equal Employment Opportunity Specialist. He developed a Navy Base civilian Training Concept with the Department Of labor, to job train individuals from the Welfare Department, Employment Development Department, who had contracts with different Training Agencies in the San Diego, Metropolitan Minority Communities to place trainees after being train into Government employment. Turning a liability to Asset person into employment, Thus saving the United States $37,000,000 in Federal Funds

After his Federal retirement. Ray has been an Adviser to Congressman Duncan Hunter ® Randy (Duke) Cunningham ® and Newt Gingrich, former Speaker of the House of Congress. He has also met privately with two Presidents of the United States of America, Richard Nixon and Ronald Reagan and has made two recommendations to Congress through Congressman Duncan Hunter, Ray developed the Concept to use the

United States Military at the Mexican Border and the use of the all weather
AWAC radar aircraft to prevent small aircraft from entering from Mexico
with drugs to the United States. Ray was employed by the United States Navy
as a civilian employee for thirty four years. He held positions as an Aircraft
Painter, Equal Employment Opportunity Committee Counselor, and Equal
Employment Opportunity Specialist, GS-11. Do to the dedication to the
Navy at United States Air Station, North Island, San Diego, as Affirmative
Action Officer. Ray earned twenty eight State of California, awards from
the City of San Diego, American GI Forum, Department of Labor and
the Navy. Ray was ask to run for the United States Congress twice by the
National Republican Committee in Washington. After his retirement from
the Federal Government (thirty four years) He went to work for General
Dynamics, Convair Division in San Diego, California. He was awarded
five outstanding Awards for his contribution in developing cost affective
procedures to get the aircraft fuselages of the MD-11 ahead of schedule.
Ray is retired now, an lives in Henderson, Nevada.

Ray's Book Summary

Ray Chavarria's Indian Roots book is about his Indian Ancestry. How he became aware in his latter years of his Indian linage. How the United States Government furnished the Documents to prove his Indian ancestry (Apache) and how latter they deny their own records. He writes concerning his Child hood life, as a teenager and adult life. His mistreatment by his own Father and Stepmother.

He tells about his Pachuco era in the 1941, the fighting and his drinking at age twelve (12). How he overcame from being an alcoholic at age 15 ½. How his wife's parents guided him as a teenager to become a better person and leave his bad habits aside. And latter his own wife provides the direction to a better life on this earth. He tells of his deep hurt in his heart for many years and the help he is getting from his closes friend Evelia Delayo to continue in his life and to forgive his enemies. And to continue finishing his Family History book. The book is base on truth and fact for the reader to learn early Indian history.